The Educator's Guide to Linguistics

The Educator's Guide to Linguistics

Tatiana Gordon

Hofstra University

INFORMATION AGE PUBLISHING, INC.
Charlotte, NC • www.infoagepub.com

Library of Congress Cataloging-in-Publication Data

Gordon, Tatiana, 1956-
  The educator's guide to linguistics / Tatiana Gordon.
      p. cm.
  Includes bibliographical references.
  ISBN 978-1-61735-880-7 (pbk.) – ISBN 978-1-61735-881-4 – ISBN
  978-1-61735-882-1 (e-book) 1. Linguistics–Study and teaching–Textbooks.
  2. Language and languages–Study and teaching–Textbooks. I. Title.
  P53.412.G66 2012
  410–dc23

                                                            2012020190

Printed in the United States of America

Contents

Preface

When a linguistics professor mentions her job, she is likely to hear something like the following: "You teach linguistics? I took Linguistics 101. Those sentence trees were awful." Even language education students often find linguistic theory abstract and hard to understand. Unfortunately, this means that linguistic findings that have the potential to transform classroom practice often remain untapped by practitioners. This book is an attempt to address this issue. It was conceived as an instructional tool for teachers and education students, one that would provide them with an accessible overview of linguistic research and explicitly discuss its instructional significance.

Many chapters in the book begin with the question, "Have you ever noticed that…?" Such references to the reader's own language experience are strategic. Starting with the familiar—the staple of effective teaching—makes the subject less intimidating and ensures that readers develop a firm and lasting grasp of new ideas. In the same vein, the book illustrates theoretical concepts with language samples (such as popular song lyrics or famous sayings) that are likely to be familiar to the reader. Ultimately, the use of such recognizable language material is intended to help students see the language in their own environment as worth observing and analyzing.

"Arbitrariness," "allophones," "agreement." Novices tend to struggle with these and a number of other concepts. Accordingly, this book uses pedagogical tools such as analogies, word-form analyses, and graphics to clarify their meaning. In a number of instances, the text tells the story of

The Educator's Guide to Linguistics, pages ix–x
Copyright © 2012 by Information Age Publishing
All rights of reproduction in any form reserved.

a linguistic discovery in some detail. Pavlov's dogs have become proverbial for a reason: When students are able to envision an experiment or follow a scientist on a field trip, they are more likely to understand a research accomplishment.

Above all, the book is meant to help future teachers in the classroom. This goal largely determines the book's scope. The text provides an overview of those studies that have especially significant implications for classroom practice. For instance, the chapter on neurolinguistics covers research into the gestures that accompany speech, and the chapter on semantics places special emphasis on discussing the role of conceptual metaphors in cognition.

Each of the book's 11 chapters concludes with a section titled "Implications for Instruction." These sections suggest follow-up activities that explore the practical significance of the research discussed in the chapter. Is it possible to overcome the arbitrariness of the linguistic sign? What language-teaching strategies are most brain-compatible? Guiding questions such as these, together with samples of innovative practices, help the reader link linguistic theory to language-teaching practice.

To avoid gender bias and to ensure a smooth read, the pronouns *he* and *she* are used interchangeably throughout the text.

—**Tatiana Gordon**

1

The Uniqueness of Language

Semiotic Properties of Language

People have always been fascinated by their language ability. According to the Judeo-Christian doctrine, language has a divine origin. In France, Spain, Russia, and a number of other countries, people tend to find their national language to be singularly expressive and beautiful. In the Muslim world, Classical Arabic is revered as a sacred tongue. Tamils in the south of India worship their language as a deity.

What do scholars have to say on the subject of language exceptionality? Scientifically speaking, is language a unique phenomenon and, if so, what is special about it? Answers to these questions are provided by *semiotics*, the research field that investigates the various systems of communication.

The unit of analysis in semiotics is the *sign*, an entity that stands for something else. Here is a sampling of various linguistic and nonlinguistic signs:

- Words (both oral and written);
- Graphic signs (e.g., icons, road signs, emblems);
- Facial expressions (e.g., a smile, a furrowed brow);

The Educator's Guide to Linguistics, pages 1–14
Copyright © 2012 by Information Age Publishing
All rights of reproduction in any form reserved.

- Gestures (e.g., a waving hand, a peace sign);
- Body language (e.g., standing at attention, bowing); and
- Animal language (e.g., postures, calls, scents).

Each item on the previous list stands for something; each one has a meaning. A road sign, like the one shown in Figure 1.1, lets you know that there is a bend in the road ahead. A waving hand signifies a greeting. By smiling, you let others know that your disposition is friendly. A cat arching its back says, "Get out of my way!"

Semiotic studies compare and contrast signs like the one in Figure 1.1. Scholars investigate the question, Do all signs work equally well, or could it be that some of them do a better job of transmitting meaning?

Research has demonstrated that language is an extraordinary system of communication. Linguistic signs have several features that are hardly ever found in nonlinguistic semiotic systems and that render communication by means of language singularly effective. So, what are these unique features of language?

First of all, linguistic signs are *arbitrary*. In semiotics, the term "arbitrary" means that the form of a sign is independent of its meaning. Words are arbitrary signs because, aside from convention, there is no reason why a certain word label is attached to a certain meaning. What you are reading right now is called a *book* in English, *hon* in Japanese, *livre* in French, and *kitab* in Arabic. You see that the form of the word meaning "book" can vary infinitely. Because word form is independent of word meaning, virtually any configuration of sounds is possible. To be sure, there do exist a few words (e.g., *howl*, *meow*, and *screech*) whose form is not arbitrary. In the case of these nonarbitrary signs, the form imitates what the word stands for. These

Figure 1.1 "Curve Ahead" road sign.

onomatopoeic words, however, are an exception to the general rule of the arbitrariness of the linguistic sign.

Nonlinguistic systems of communication often work differently. Take, for instance, the road sign "Curve Ahead" shown in Figure 1.1. This graphic sign is not an arbitrary configuration of lines. Rather, it is an image of a bending road. For the graphic sign to work, its form must resemble its meaning.

Like graphic signs, gestures and body language are seldom arbitrary. Consider the open hand we wave in greeting. According to one theory, this gesture was originally used to let others know that an individual was unarmed. A waving hand is thus not the mere product of an arbitrary convention: there is a link between this sign's form and its meaning.

Animal language is also rarely arbitrary. An angry cat arches its back for a reason: an arched back makes its body look larger. This stance suggests strength and the ability to put up a fight.

But is the arbitrariness of language a good thing? On the one hand, arbitrariness can be inconvenient. Because nothing about word form suggests word meaning, words are hard to remember. On the other hand, arbitrariness makes language a powerful communication tool. Because we are not restricted by the need to custom fit word form to word meaning, we are able to give a name to any meaning, no matter how elaborate or abstract it may be. Humans have thus been able to come up with sophisticated words such as *education, existentialism, catharsis,* and thousands of others. Nonlinguistic signs, such as a gesture or a graphic sign, are less likely to convey elaborate abstract concepts. Just try creating a gesture or a graphic sign that means "irony" or "sentence," and you will see for yourself that nonlinguistic signs are no match to words.

Another unique property of language is its *duality of patterning.* The term "duality" suggests that language has two levels. There is a primary level of sounds, a limited set of small units devoid of their own meaning. These sounds, meaningless by themselves, are combined on the secondary level, the meaningful level of words. Thus, in any language, the meaningless building blocks of a few sounds are configured into many meaningful word signs. While the number of sounds we can produce is restricted by the anatomy of the vocal tract, the number of words that can be created out of these few sounds is virtually without limit. English, for instance, has just over 30 sounds, with the exact number depending on the individual dialect. Out of these 30 or so sounds, countless words have been made. The complete *Oxford English Dictionary,* for instance, lists over 400,000 entries!

No other system of communication, besides language, has dual patterning. It is impossible to analyze gestures, facial expressions, or animal language into a limited number of clear-cut, distinct building blocks.

Duality of patterning makes language a superior system of communication. Imagine what our language would be like if it were *not* dually patterned. The number of words in such a language would not exceed the number of sounds we were physically able to produce. Picture a language in which the sound *f* means "food," *d* stands for "drink," and so on, with the total number of words being about 30. Not a very effective communication system, is it? And yet, this is exactly how animal languages work. In these languages, each individual sound is a "word," a signal that means "danger" or "territory." The number of these signals is severely limited by the anatomy of animals' vocal tracts, with most species averaging from three to six distinct sounds.

An analogy further clarifies the benefit offered by a dually patterned communication system. Imagine two individuals who enjoy making models. While one of them owns Lego blocks, the other can only work with a few monolithic rocks. You will undoubtedly agree that the model maker who has Lego blocks at his disposal has an advantage, since blocks provide for a more flexible building material. It may be helpful to think of language as an ever-growing, ever-expanding edifice made out of the small building blocks of sounds.

Another useful property of languages is *open-endedness*. This term refers to languages' limitless capacity for growing. New words and phrases are being coined every day in every language. Over recent years, for instance, scores of new words, such as *facebook, twitter,* and *blog* have cropped up in everyday English. Because of our language's open-endedness, we are free to come up with any number of new subjects to talk about. The progress of science and the evolution of society are made possible by our ability to say new things.

Open-endedness is a unique property of human language not found in the animal world. No animal is able to create a single new sign, and the language of an animal species does not change over time.

An interesting experiment performed by Austrian scholar Karl von Frisch demonstrated the lack of open-endedness in animal language. Von Frisch studied bees, known to have a complex system of communication. When scout bees spot nectar, they return to their hive and relay the news about their find. Scout bees communicate by performing a dance. The speed and the orientation of the dance convey two separate meanings: where the nectar is located in relation to the hive, and how far from the hive it is. In other words, bee language has signals for direction on a horizontal plane and also for distance. In his experiment, von Frisch placed a jar with some sweet syrup on top of a 20-foot-tall pole—much higher than where bees normally collect their nectar. Scout bees spotted the jar and returned to the hive with the good news. Gatherer bees duly flew in the direction of the pole. However, upon reaching their destination, instead of going to the top of the pole, the gatherer bees just kept flying around chaotically. Why didn't they go for the jar? The scout bees, whose system of communication is closed, had failed to come up with just a single sign: "up"!

Another property of language that distinguishes it from other semiotic systems is *displacement*, or the ability to describe things outside of the here and now. Due to languages' capacity for displacement, we have absolutely no difficulty in talking about things removed from us in time and space— or even things that are imaginary. We can, for instance, describe the time when dinosaurs roamed the earth or project what life will be like a million years from now.

Displacement is only found in human language. Animals communicate exclusively about their immediate environment. A dog is able to convey the message "I am hungry," but it cannot say, "I am full now, but, yesterday, I did not have a bite to eat and felt really famished." Similarly, a cat can let you know "I love my kittens," but it cannot announce, "I think I am going to make a nurturing parent."

Finally, language is characterized by *stimulus-freedom*. This term refers to the fact that human speech can be independent of its context. Neither external environments nor our internal dispositions necessarily compel us to say anything in particular. Thus, you can feel livid about a situation and yet utter, with perfect amiability, "Isn't that lovely!" Language's stimulus-freedom gives you the choice to say anything you wish. It is not so in the animal world. In animal language, the instincts prompt the production of a signal, with certain stimuli inevitably entailing certain calls, scents, or postures.

You now know some major ways in which human language is distinct from other systems of communication. It is arbitrary, dually patterned, and open ended. It has the capacity for displacement and being used independently of context. Our use of a communication system characterized by these unique properties defines us as humans. But why is it that humans have this powerful instrument of communication, and other animal species do not? The answer to this question is discussed next.

The Language Instinct

Some scholars espouse innatism, the belief that language is wired into our genes and that human babies enter the world with a natural propensity for language learning. This belief is known as the innateness hypothesis.

An analogy may help the reader appreciate the main thrust of the innatist view of language. Consider some human skills, such as dancing, sewing, and wrestling. These skills are *not* innate. Learning them takes special aptitude, concerted effort, and at the very least a little bit of instruction. These skills do not develop out of biological necessity, as may be seen from the plain fact that many humans do not know how to dance, sew, or wrestle!

In contrast, some other skills, such as sucking and walking, are part of the human genetic program. All healthy humans are able to suck when they are born and to walk starting around their first birthday. From the innatist perspective, language acquisition is similar to babies learning how to nurse and toddlers learning how to walk. These skills develop naturally, provided children are exposed to the relevant stimuli. Innatists use the term *language instinct* to refer to the human ability for language learning.

The innateness hypothesis was formulated in the mid-1960s by an American linguist of German extraction, Eric Lenneberg. Lenneberg studied various kinds of innate skills and came up with a set of criteria that apply to *all* of them. According to Lenneberg, (1) innate skills are developed instinctively, so that learning a particular skill cannot be avoided; (2) innate skills are developed following a rigid and predictable schedule; and (3) there is an optimal period for mastering innate skills: if they are learned outside this period, they fail to develop properly. Lenneberg argued that human language ability meets these essential criteria for innateness.

While the genetic program for language has not as yet been found, a significant body of nongenetic research does provide indirect evidence that our language ability is indeed congenital.

The Critical Period Hypothesis

Research data pertaining to the first two criteria of innateness are discussed later, in Chapter 7 of this book. In this chapter, we consider the third criterion. We examine the evidence that language can only be learned during the early period of human life.

The optimal stage for developing any innate skill is known as the *critical period*. During the critical period, the organism is particularly sensitive to certain stimuli, and the skill in question is bound to develop. If, however, for some reason, stimuli are not provided at the right time, and if learning takes place at a later stage, the innate skill fails to develop normally. No amount of instruction will make a difference. Once the window of opportunity closes, it is impossible to make up for the lost time.

An example of a congenital skill learned during a critical period is bird singing. Zebra finches, for instance, can only master their song immediately after hatching. It is of crucial importance that fledglings be able to hear adult song early on. Young finches whose exposure to adults' singing was experimentally delayed never mastered all the complexities of finch song.

Innatists believe that, like any innate skill, language can only be learned during a critical period. They theorize that if, for some reason, a child has been deprived of early exposure to language, the language instinct is not triggered, the window of opportunity closes, and the child fails to master language. This hypothesis is known as the *critical period hypothesis*.[1]

You are probably wondering if the critical period hypothesis has ever been tested. Obviously, nobody has ever attempted to check this theory by depriving children of exposure to language. However, in some tragic cases, children have been raised without being spoken to. These situations, which can be thought of as inadvertent experiments, have enabled scholars to observe what happens when a child misses out on the critical period for language learning. One such incident happened in the United States.

In 1970, a woman walked into a welfare office in a small town in Los Angeles County. The woman led a little girl by the hand. Something about the way the girl looked alarmed the office staff. Social workers were dispatched to the girl's home. They were appalled by what they discovered. It turned out that Genie—such was the pseudonym given to the girl to protect her identity—had been severely abused by her deranged father. Until this time, the girl had lived in virtual confinement in a small room. All day, she had been made to sit on a potty. Genie had been completely deprived of child or adult company and had received practically no exposure to speech. Whenever she cried or made any other noise, Genie's father had punished her. Genie's mother never dared to oppose her husband. At the time when she was discovered, Genie had very little language.

Genie was promptly removed from her home and placed in foster care. A team of counselors and therapists proceeded to work on her rehabilitation. Scholars and educators wondered what language development was going to be like in a child who had missed out on the window of opportunity for language learning. The outcome of Genie's story was sad. Even though she developed significant vocabulary, Genie never fully mastered language.

Genie's control of grammar was particularly limited. At the age of 13, Genie produced sentences such as *Fred have feel good* or *Where is tomorrow Mrs. L.*

Those unfortunate boys and girls who, like Genie, have been deprived of early exposure to language are known as *feral children* (from the Latin *ferus*, meaning "wild"). Among those to have suffered a similar fate were two Indian girls, Amala and Kamala, reportedly found in the jungle in the 1920s; a French boy, Victor, known as the "wild boy of Aveyron," found in the south of France in the 1790s; and Chelsea, an American. All of these children having, for one reason or another, missed out on early exposure to language, none of them was able to make up for the lost time. No amount of instruction made a difference in these feral children's language attainment. Even though some of them mastered vocabulary to a reasonable extent, none attained a full control of grammar.

The evidence gained from cases of feral children is crucial. Many scientists today believe that the mother tongue can only be fully learned during the early years of human life. It is believed that the window of opportunity for language learning closes, and the language instinct wanes, around the age of puberty.

Universal Grammar Hypothesis

But which aspects of language are innate? A notable attempt to answer this question was made by MIT scholar Noam Chomsky, one of the most frequently cited scholars of all time. The theory developed by Chomsky has had an enormous impact. In the late 1950s and early 1960s, when Chomsky's studies of language first came out, they unleashed violent debates that came to be known as the "linguistics wars." Generations of linguists have been busy testing Chomsky's hypothesis. What are the ideas that stirred this intellectual commotion?

Like Lenneberg, Chomsky believes that human language ability is innate. However, he has taken Lenneberg's argument a step farther. Chomsky has been impressed by the facility and creativity children display when acquiring grammar. He has pointed out that children as young as 3 or 4 years intuitively know the basic rules of sentence formation. Moreover, children do not just copy sentences used by adults. Rather, young children are able to produce grammatically correct sentences they have never heard before.

According to Chomsky, children's ease in mastering grammar is all the more surprising given that children's exposure to language is limited. The language children use as material for inferring the rules of grammar is messy, full of false starts and interruptions. Somehow, out of this imperfect, limited input, children are able to extricate the entire set of grammatical rules. Chomsky's contention that the language children are exposed to is insufficient for the full mastery of grammar is known as the *poverty of stimulus* or *dearth of input* argument.

Chomsky hypothesized that children are facile grammar learners because their grammatical development ability is innate. According to this theory, known as the *Universal Grammar hypothesis*, a grammatical blueprint is prewired into children's brains. This does not mean, of course, that babies are born with the knowledge that the ending -*s*, for instance, is a plurality marker in English. Such language-specific rules, part of the vastly varied surface structure of language, cannot possibly be innate. What may be innate, however, is the so-called deep structure, which incorporates the universal grammatical features of all languages. All languages, for instance, have phrase structure; in all languages, a sentence is made of a noun phrase and a verb phrase. It is these universal grammatical features that are congenital, according to Chomsky.

Using a rather technological, 1960s-style metaphor, Chomsky further argued that children are endowed with a language organ or *language acquisition device* (LAD). The LAD becomes activated or turns on when children are exposed to language stimuli. According to this theory, the LAD enables children to produce sentences that comply with the rules of Universal Grammar.

Not all linguists are in agreement with Chomsky's position. Some contend that the facts of language learning do not bear out his theory. For instance, Harvard psychologist Catherine Snow has pointed out that the language to which children are exposed is not impoverished and ungrammatical. Snow and some other linguists who have been observing adult-child interaction report that caretakers use a special kind of language when talking to babies. This language, known as *motherese*, is slow, repetitive, and grammatically correct. According to Snow, exposure to motherese provides small children with something like a grammar lesson.[2]

Nicaraguan Sign Language and the Creolization of Pidgins

On the other hand, evidence in support of Chomsky's theory has been provided by two fascinating studies. One was conducted in Nicaragua.

During the Somoza dictatorship, a small school for the deaf was founded by Hope Somoza, the dictator's wife. In 1979, after the Sandinista revolution toppled Somoza's regime, the school was expanded; special efforts were made to teach the deaf children how to read lips. Since lip-reading lessons are seldom successful, the children unsurprisingly did not make much progress and remained unable to communicate. Before long, however, the teachers noticed that the deaf children had come up with their own solution to the problem at hand. They were using gestures to interact with each other.

The Nicaraguan teachers invited an MIT linguist, Judy Kegl, to study this sign language. Kegl realized that the children did not gesture randomly. Rather, their signing followed certain rules. The children had developed these rules of grammar entirely from scratch.[3]

Today, the system of communication created by the Nicaraguan deaf children is officially recognized as Nicaraguan Sign Language (NSL). Interestingly enough, Kegl has reported on a group of adults who had little difficulty in learning the NSL vocabulary, but were unable to attain full mastery of its grammar. Apparently, these adult learners had missed out on the window of opportunity for learning NSL!

The case of Nicaraguan Sign Language has demonstrated that, in the absence of exposure to grammatically structured speech, children proceed to create their own grammar. Many scholars believe that the Nicaraguan deaf children's instinctive grammatical creativity supports the Universal Grammar Hypothesis. The children could not help creating a grammar because they were biologically programmed to do so.

Further evidence in support of the Universal Grammar hypothesis has been provided by studies of *pidgins*. Pidgin languages arise in the situations of language contact when speakers of different languages who do not have a language in common need to communicate with each other. Pidgins were used by slaves and slave traders on Caribbean plantations and in Papua New Guinea. When people from around the word went to work in Hawaii, they too interacted in pidgin.

Pidgin languages share several characteristics. Pidgin vocabularies are made of a small number of nouns, verbs, and adjectives borrowed from languages spoken in the area of contact. These vocabularies are just big enough to meet people's basic communication needs. Pidgin grammars are rudimentary. Their verbs don't have tense markers, and their nouns lack plural forms. Functional words, such as pronouns, prepositions, or conjunctions, are practically nonexistent. Pidgins also lack strict rules of word order. Because pidgins do not have developed grammars, each speaker of a pidgin uses the language slightly differently. There are no native speakers of pidgins. These languages are learned in adulthood.

In areas of language contact, children speak a variety of different languages at home. When playing with each other, however, they use pidgins.

An American scholar of pidgins, Derek Bickerton, reports that something quite remarkable happens when children converse in a pidgin.[4] Instead of merely reproducing the language patterns used by adults, children infuse complex grammatical structures into the structurally impoverished contact languages. The languages that arise in pidgin-speaking communities are called *creoles*. Learned in childhood, creoles are such children's native languages. Each new generation of Creole-speaking children expands the given language's repertoire of grammatical forms until it becomes a fully developed linguistic system. Haitian Creole, an official language of Haiti, is an example of a Creole language that evolved from a pidgin. Creoles have striking grammatical similarities.

Since Creole grammars are created by children, *creolization of pidgin*, the process whereby pidgins develop into Creoles, is viewed as proof of the validity of the Universal Grammar hypothesis.

The Origins of Language

Language is a unique system of communication that sets human beings apart from other species. But when and how did language arise? Unfortunately, scientists have no early language data to work with, and theories of the origins of language are largely speculative. They are often mentioned under facetious nicknames coined by Danish linguist Otto Jespersen.

According to the "bow-wow" theory, language originated when humans began to imitate sounds in their environment, especially animal calls. According to this theory, onomatopoeic signs similar to words such as *crash*, *bang*, and *meow* were the precursors of language. Working against this theory, however, is the fact that words for natural sounds are few and vastly different in different languages.

According to the "pooh-pooh" theory, language evolved from involuntary cries and exclamations such as *ouch* and *ha-ha-ha*. This theory is not entirely plausible either, though, because interjections make up only a small set of words in any language.

Yet another theory, the "yo-he-ho" theory, claims that language arose out of vocalizations uttered during physical labor. According to this belief, the rhythmical chants that accompanied communal work were the seeds out of which language eventually grew. The rhythmic nature of any language lends some credibility to this theory. Still, at this point, there is no explanation for how full-fledged language could have evolved out of rhythmic grunts.

Jespersen himself espoused a more romantic theory of language origin. According to his "la-la" theory, language sprang from the noises made during courtship. This theory, too, has a gap in it. Tracing the origin of language to emotional cries does not account for its rational aspects.

When language originated also remains unknown. Many scientists believe that hominids had evolved a vocal tract and a nervous system that made language possible by around 50,000–20,000 B.C.

Implications for Instruction

1. Recall that, because of the arbitrariness of language, new words are hard to remember. Luckily, teachers can do something to make language less arbitrary. Word retention is facilitated when the learning of new words is accompanied by a hand gesture that illustrates the word's meaning. What gestures could you use in the classroom to teach words of motion, such as *twirl*, *skip*, and *bounce?* Create gestures to facilitate the retention of scientific terms, such as *electricity* and *gravity.*

2. Because of language's open-endedness, people continuously create new words to name new things and express new ideas. Below is a list of some new English words that have been coined over recent years. Discuss whether you would teach these words to language learners. Create mini-activities with the focus on these or other recent neologisms.

   1995: *Web*

   1996: *mom* (as in *soccer mom*)

   2001: *9-11*

   2003: *metrosexual*

   2008: *bailout* (a rescue by government of a failing corporation)

WORDS TO REMEMBER

semiotics: the study of communication systems.

sign: a unit of analysis in semiotics; an entity that stands for something else.

arbitrariness: in semiotics, the lack of a connection between a sign's form and its meaning.

duality of patterning: the sign structure whereby a few entities that are themselves void of meaning are combined into meaningful entities.

open-endedness: in semiotics, this term refers to a language's capacity to evolve.

displacement: in semiotics, this term refers to language's capacity to describe things beyond the here and now.

stimulus-freedom: refers to the human ability to use language independent of context.

innateness hypothesis: the belief that human language ability is congenital.

language instinct: the human capacity for language learning, believed to be innate.

critical period: the optimal period for learning a congenital skill.

critical period hypothesis: the belief that language can only be fully developed in childhood.

feral children: children who did not receive exposure to language during the critical period and who have thus suffered from abnormal language development.

Universal Grammar hypothesis: the belief that humans are endowed with a congenital blueprint for acquiring grammar.

poverty of stimulus argument: an argument that children's exposure to language is limited and does not provide sufficient material for inferring the entire set of grammar rules.

dearth of input argument: see **poverty of stimulus argument**.

motherese: language used by mothers for interacting with babies.

Nicaraguan Sign Language: a grammatically structured sign language developed by deaf children in Nicaragua.

pidgin: a rudimentary system of communication used by adults in the absence of a common language.

creole: languages that evolve in areas of contact.

creolization of pidgins: the process whereby pidgins evolve into creoles.

Notes

1. Lenneberg, E. H. (1967). *Biological foundations of language.* New York: Wiley.
2. Snow, C. E. (1972). Mothers' speech to children learning language. *Child Development, 43,* 549–565.

3. Kegl, J. (1994). The Nicaraguan Sign Language project: An overview. *Signpost, 7*(1), 24–31.

4. Bickerton, D. (1984). The language bioprogram hypothesis. *Behavioral and Brain Sciences, 7,* 173–221.

2

Speech Sounds

Phonetics and Phonology

This chapter provides an introduction to the science of speech sounds. The two disciplines that study the sounds of speech are *phonetics* and *phonology*. The primary concern of phonetics is with studying the acoustic properties of speech sounds, as well as the organs involved in speech-sound production and perception.

As for phonology, it studies speech sounds as a system. Phonological studies have provided an important insight: languages are not random collections of sounds. Rather, the sounds of each language are organized into a coherent system of which speakers have intuitive knowledge.

This chapter mostly discusses the sounds of Northern American English (NAE), although it also mentions some sounds from other languages.

In this chapter, you are introduced to the system of speech-sound notation known as the phonetic alphabet. Transcribing speech by means of the phonetic alphabet provides scholars with a way of recording sounds that is free of the inconsistencies inherent in spelling.

The Educator's Guide to Linguistics, pages 15–31
Copyright © 2012 by Information Age Publishing
All rights of reproduction in any form reserved.

Initiation, Articulation, and Voicing

We start by discussing the organs of speech; that is, the parts of your body involved in making speech sounds. You can think of your speech organs as a sound-making instrument. The instrument is made of bellows (the lungs and the bronchi), various pipes (the trachea and the larynx), chambers of different sizes and shapes (the mouth and nasal cavities), and numerous valves (e.g., the vocal cords, the tongue, the teeth, and the lips). When you make speech sounds, you blow air with the bellows of the lungs and bronchi through the pipes of the trachea and larynx into the mouth or nasal chambers and manipulate the airstream with an array of valves: the vocal cords, the tongue, the teeth, and the lips.

Getting the air to move is crucial for speech production. Because, like any other sound, a speech sound is a vibration of the air, you need *initiation* to set the air in motion. To understand the critical role of initiation for making speech sounds, try speaking while holding your breath. It is impossible to achieve this feat.

Egressive pulmonic air—that is, the air that escapes from our lungs—is used for producing most speech sounds in NAE. Sometimes, however, speech sounds are made with ingressive pulmonic air, or the air that we breathe in. This happens when we speak while laughing or sobbing.

The shaping of the airstream with the help of articulators (the valve-like organs) is called articulation. Articulators can create a complete or almost complete obstruction of the airstream. This type of articulation produces *consonants.* Alternatively, articulators can let the airstream pass relatively unimpeded, resulting in the production of *vowels.*

To observe the difference in articulation between vowels and consonants, perform an experiment. Pronounce the consonant "ffff," noting the obstruction of the airstream created by the lower lip and upper teeth. Now say the vowel "eeeeee" and observe the free passage of air through the mouth cavity.

Some English consonants are *voiced* (e.g., [b], [g], [d], and [z]), whereas others are *voiceless* (e.g., [p], [k], [t], [s], and [h]). How is voicing created? Put your hand on the front of your throat. Do you feel a bump? That's a piece of cartilage called the Adam's apple. (It is larger in men than in women.) The Adam's apple protects the larynx, a pipe-like structure. The larynx holds the *vocal cords,* two bands of muscle running horizontally from the front to the back of the larynx (see Figure 2.1). The space between the vocal cords, called the glottis, can be closed or opened together with the

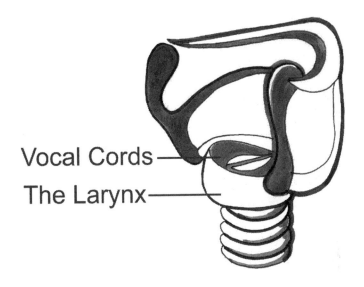

Figure 2.1   The larynx.

vocal cords. Voicing happens when the stream of moving air hits the closed glottis, causing the vocal cords to vibrate.

To observe how vocal cords work, perform an experiment. Once again, put your hand on your Adam's apple; this time, make a "zzzz" sound. Do you feel the vibration of the vocal cords? It is that vibration that lends voice to the voiced speech sounds. Now say "sss." Observe that your vocal cords are not engaged in the production of voiceless sounds.

While the consonants of NAE can be both voiced and voiceless, its vowels are normally voiced. In contrast, some languages (e.g., Japanese and Portuguese) have voiceless vowels. In Japanese, vowels are voiceless (or pronounced with a whispery voice) when they occur between voiceless consonants. Thus, the *u* sound in the word *Sukida!* ("I like it!") is voiceless. To experience the voiceless Japanese vowels, say *Sukida!*, pronouncing the underlined vowels with a "whispery" voice.

Consonants

Consonants are grouped based on two parameters: the *place* and the *manner* of their articulation. Let us now talk about the eight major places of articulation for the NAE consonants, starting with the lips and moving all the way down to the glottis.

The NAE consonants [b], [p], [m], and [w] are produced with both lips. These consonants are *bilabial*.

The consonants [f] and [v] are articulated with the upper teeth and the lower lip. They are *labiodental* consonants.

The consonants [ð] and [θ] in the words *the* and *thick* are articulated with the tongue thrust between the teeth. These consonants are *interdental.*

Right behind your teeth, there is a bump called the alveolar ridge. The English consonants [t], [d], [s], [n], [z], [l], [ʃ] as in *shine*, [ʒ] as in genre, [tʃ] as in *chair*, and [dʒ] as in *job*, are pronounced with the tip of the tongue touching the alveolar ridge. These consonants are *alveolar.*

The first sound of the word *right*, transcribed with the [ɹ] symbol, is articulated with the tongue curled backward, past the alveolar ridge. This type of articulation is called *retroflex.*

The sound [j] as in *yoke* is articulated behind the alveolar ridge by the contact of the back of the tongue with the hard palate (the roof of your mouth). This sound is *palatal.*

Now, run your finger along the hard palate on the roof of your mouth. (Make sure you don't reach too far, so as not to gag.) As you move your finger backward, you will feel the soft sagging tissue where the roof of the mouth slopes down. That tissue is the velum or the soft palate. The English consonants [k], [g], and [ŋ] as in *ring*—all made by the contact of the back of the tongue with the velum—are *velar.*

Pronouncing the English consonant [h] as in *hoe* involves pushing the airstream through the narrowed glottis. Say the word *hoe* and note the constriction of the glottis involved in making the [h] sound. The English sound [h] is *glottal.*

Now, let us examine the *ways* in which consonants can be articulated. The air obstruction involved in articulating consonants can be complete, partial, complete-with-partial, and loose. Let us consider these four types of obstruction in detail.

The sounds articulated with complete obstruction of the air passage are called *stops.* The English sounds [p], [b], [t], [d], [k], and [g] are stops. Pronounce the sounds [p] and [b] and observe the complete closure involved in their articulation.

Articulators can also produce only a partial closure, leaving an opening through which air escapes with a great deal of friction. Sounds produced in this manner are called *fricatives.* Say "sssss" and observe the accompanying air friction. The English sounds [f], [v], [s], [z], [h], [ð] as in *then*, [θ] as in thick, [ʃ] as in *share*, and [ʒ] as in genre, are fricatives.

Another group of sounds, called *affricates*, start as stops and terminate as fricatives. The English sounds [tʃ], as in <u>ch</u>air, and [dʒ], as in *job*, are affricates.

In another group of consonants, called *approximants*, the articulators come close together, but not close enough to create either total air stoppage or air friction. In approximants, the air escapes freely through the obstruction created by the articulators. The English approximants are the sounds [m], [w], [n], [l], [ɹ], [ŋ] as in *reading*, and [j] as in *yes*.

Table 2.1 summarizes the NAE consonants according to the eight places and four types of their articulation.

Vowels voiced

The quality of the vowel sound depends, first and foremost, on how the tongue shapes the airstream within the mouth cavity. Let us now perform two experiments to observe the tongue position involved in the articulation of vowels. The first experiment focuses on the horizontal movement of the tongue. Pronounce the vowel [i] as in *see* and then the vowel [u] as in *who*. Prolong the "eee" and the "ooo" and observe the tongue positions involved. Note that when you articulate [i], the body of the tongue is thrust forward with the tongue resting against the lower teeth. When you pronounce the [u] in *who*, the tongue is bunched up and pulled back.

Now let us observe the height of the tongue. Say the [i] in <u>see</u> and the [æ] in <u>cat</u>, prolonging the vowels and paying attention to your tongue and jaw movement. Note that when you say [i], the tongue is higher and when you say [æ], the tongue lies lower in the mouth cavity and the jaw is dropped.

TABLE 2.1 NAE Consonants

	Bi labial	Labio dental	Inter dental	Alveolar	Retroflex	Palatal	Velar	Glottal
Stop	p b			t d			k g	
Fricative		f v	θ ð	s z ʃ ʒ				h
Affricate				tʃ dʒ				
Approximant	m w			n l	ɹ	j	ŋ	

Let us summarize the results of these two experiments. Depending on how far forward or backward the tongue is, NAE vowels can be front or back; depending on the height of the tongue, they can be high or low. There are also vowels with in-between tongue positions. Those that are neither front nor back are central; those that are neither high nor low are mid. Table 2.2 summarizes the six tongue positions for the NAE vowels.

Note the eight shaded boxes in Table 2.2. The shaded areas depict four vowel pairs that have similar articulations: [i] and [ɪ] are both high and front, [u] and [ʊ] are high and back, [e] and [ɛ] are mid-front, and [o] and [ɔ] are mid-back. While the two members of each pair have articulations similar to each other, there is, in every case, an important point of difference between them. In all four cases, the first member of the pair is tense and the second one is lax.

The tense vowels in *see*, *boo*, *bay*, and *no* are sometimes described as "long." The term "tense" is more accurate, though, because these vowels are not necessarily long. Rather, they are pronounced with significant muscular tension of the tongue, in contrast to their lax counterparts popularly known as "short" vowels.

An experiment will help you discern the difference between tense and lax vowels. Using a high voice pitch, sing the word pairs *see* and *sit* and *bay* and *bet*. Observe the greater muscular contraction involved in the articulation of the tense vowels.

NAE also has *diphthongs*, vowels characterized by dual articulation, or a noticeable change in quality. The three NAE diphthongs are:

[aɪ] as in *pie*—low central with a high front glide;
[aʊ] as in *now*—low central with a high front glide; and
[ɔɪ] as in *boy*—low back with a high front glide.

TABLE 2.2   NAE Vowels

	Front	Central	Back	
High	i *see*		U *boo*	tense
	ɪ *sit*		ʊ *book*	lax
Mid	e *bay*	ə *above*	O *no*	tense
	ɛ *bet*	ʌ *above*	ɔ *naughty*	lax
Low	æ *bat*	a *pot*	

Note that all three NAE diphthongs start as low vowels and terminate with high glides.

Pronunciation Challenges

Some NAE pronunciation sounds present challenges to language learners. Have you ever observed native Russian speakers saying, *It is fife o'clock. I must leaf now* or *This problem is really bat*? These are examples of devoicing, or pronouncing voiceless sounds in place of voiced ones. Russian-speaking students tend to devoice voiced consonants in word-final position because, in Russian, word-final stops and fricatives are always voiceless.

Or have you ever observed English-language learners having difficulty articulating the English bilabial [w]? For instance, German and Russian students may say, *The veather vas vet* or *I drank vine.* As for Spanish-speaking students, they have difficulty with labiodental [v], for instance, realizing the word *vowel* as "bowel." Again, these errors stem from the sound patterns of the learners' home languages: the absence in German and Russian of the bilabial approximant [w] and in Spanish of the labiodental fricative [v].

Articulating the English alveolar [t] and [d] presents challenges to speakers of Bengali, Hindi, Punjabi, Urdu, and other languages of the Indian subcontinent. The problem arises because, in these languages, the *t* and *d* sounds are retroflex, not alveolar. Retroflex *t* and *d* are pronounced with the tongue curled backward, which lends r-coloring to the Hindi *t* and *d* sounds, so that they come off somewhat like *tr* or *dr*. This type of articulation is found in the Hindi words *ṭaapu* ("island") and *laḍka* ("boy"). Habits of retroflex pronunciation are very strong, and learners used to retroflex articulation may make English *t* and *d* retroflex as well.

The retroflex approximant [ɹ] is one of the hardest English sounds to master. In some languages, such as Russian and Spanish, the *r* sound is a *trill*. When the trill is articulated, the tongue taps quickly against the alveolar ridge. Speakers of Russian and Spanish often replace the English retroflex [ɹ] with a trill.

Another possible articulator for the *r* sound is the uvula, a U-shaped wedge of flesh extending from the back of the velum. (You can see the uvula in the mirror if you open your mouth really wide and hold the root of the tongue flat.) The *r* sound is uvular in Arabic and French, which is why speakers of French and Arabic often replace retroflex [ɹ] with its uvular counterpart.

Another group of students who may find the English retroflex [ɹ] hard to master includes speakers of Mandarin, Japanese, and Korean. Speakers of these languages have difficulty distinguishing between the English [ɹ] and [l] and may pronounce *arrive* as "alive" and *right* as "light."

The alveolar fricative [ʃ] may be challenging for Spanish-speaking students. Because Spanish lacks this sound, Spanish speakers tend to replace it with its closest approximation, the alveolar affricate [tʃ], producing utterances such as *I am going to sail a <u>chip</u>* or *I need to go to a <u>chop</u> to buy something.*

Another sound that is often mispronounced is the velar approximant [ŋ]. Speakers of Russian and other languages that lack the velar approximant replace it with [ng] or even [nk], for instance realizing *reading* as "readink."

The glottal, "breathy" English [h] is often articulated with the velum by speakers of some languages (e.g., Greek and Russian), resulting in a sound pronounced with greater friction.

Let us now talk about the challenges inherent in learning the NAE vowels. The tense and lax vowel pairs are particularly hard to master. The difficulty has to do with the fact that most languages have fewer vowels than English and do not make the tense-versus-lax distinction. Language learners who speak Arabic, Chinese, French, and Russian (to name just some examples) have difficulty in perceiving and producing tense and lax vowels. Some English-language learners produce vowels that are neither entirely tense nor entirely lax. Others switch tense and lax sounds, switching *greed* and *grid*, *fool* and *full*, and *peach* and *pitch*.

In sum, there are two types of pronunciation challenges. The first one has to do with the difficulty in articulation. Recall, for instance, that learners may struggle with articulating the interdentals [θ] and [ð], the bilabial [w], or the retroflex [ɹ]. The other challenge has to do with speech-sound perception, as when learners are unable to tell apart the tense [i] and the lax [ɪ]. The articulation challenge is not surprising. But why do learners have difficulty in discriminating between some target language sounds? The answer to this question—provided by the science of phonology—is discussed in the next section of this chapter.

Phonemes and Allophones

Phonology is a discipline that explores the systematic nature of speech sounds. Note that phonological transcription uses slanting lines (e.g., /p/, /b/), suggesting that a speech sound is part of a system.

Phonological studies have demonstrated that there are two kinds of speech sounds: those that do and those that do not change word meaning.

Phonemes
Changes the meaning of word

We first discuss the sounds that do cause word meaning to change. Consider the /w/ sound in _wet_. Perform a test and replace /w/ with /v/. The replacement yields a different word: _vet_. Switching /w/ to /v/ results in a change of meaning. Or, replace the tense /i/ in _beat_ with the lax /ɪ/. This switch yields the word _bit_—a different word with a different meaning.

This replacement technique is called the _minimal pair test._ A minimal pair is made of two words that are identical except for two sounds that occur in the same position. Consider some more examples:

van–ban
bat–bet
lease–leash

The minimal pair test is a procedure for identifying the meaning-changing sounds we mentioned earlier. These sounds are called _phonemes._ A phoneme can be defined as a speech sound that changes word meaning, distinguishing one word from another.

When you hear two words in a minimal pair (e.g., _sheep_ and _ship_ or _grid_ and _greed_), there is no doubt in your mind that you are dealing with two different words. However, speakers of other languages may not hear this phonemic difference. Why is that the case? Phonemes (and minimal pairs) vary from language to language. We tend to perceive foreign sounds through the phonemic filter of our home language. If a student's home language lacks a certain phonemic feature, such as, say, the tense/lax distinction, she will initially perceive the words in the tense/lax minimal pairs as being identical and will confuse them in her own speech.

To appreciate how hard it may be to tell some target-language phonemes apart, let us consider an example from Mandarin Chinese. In Chinese, as well as in other _tone languages_ (e.g., Cantonese, Vietnamese, Thai, Igbo, and Yoruba), word tone or word pitch is phonemic. Different tones change word meaning and serve to distinguish between words. Below are examples of three Mandarin Chinese words whose meanings are distinguished based on their different tones:

bā – high tone, "eight"
bá – rising tone, "to uproot," "to pull out"
bǎ – falling-and-rising tone, "to hold"

If you study Chinese, you might initially be unable to tell these three words apart just as some English language learners may be have difficulty perceiving the English phonemic distinctions.

Let us now discuss speech sounds that do not change word meaning. Consider the /t/ sound in the word *later*. Some speakers of NAE pronounce this word with a special kind of /t/ called a *flap*. A flap is a voiced sound pronounced with the tongue flicking swiftly against the alveolar ridge. When *later* is pronounced with a flap, it comes off as "lader" or "larer."

Note that replacing the voiceless /t/ with a flap does *not* change word meaning. Whether a speaker pronounces *later* with a flap or with a voiceless stop, she still says the same word. This shows that the flap is a variant of the /t/ phoneme; it is the same sound with a different pronunciation "hue." Such speech sounds with alternative pronunciation hues are *allophones*. Allophones are defined as speech-sound variants that do not change word meaning.

Let us consider some more examples of allophones. Take the word *pop*. This word contains two allophones of /p/. The initial /p/ is aspirated; it is pronounced with a puff of air. The final /p/ is unaspirated. An experiment demonstrates the difference between the aspirated and unaspirated /p/ allophones. Say *pop* while holding your hand in front of your mouth. Observe that the puff of air is only there when you say the initial /p/.

Alternative allophonic pronunciations are often determined by the sound's position in a word. Flap, for instance, only happens between vowels. Aspirated /p/ occurs in word-initial position; its unaspirated allophone is used in word-final position. Thus, allophones are often (but not always) positional variants of phonemes.

Phonotactics

Language sounds are not combined randomly. Strict rules prescribe the sound sequences that are possible or impossible in a given language. There are, for instance, rules that dictate which sound clusters may occur at the beginning of a word. In English, words cannot begin with the sound cluster [kn]. However, words with the initial [kn] cluster do occur in Hebrew (e.g., *Knesset*) and Norwegian (e.g., *Knut*).

The area of linguistics that describes sound combinations is called *phonotactics*. A phonotactic rule dictates that English can have up to three consonants in word-initial position. Take the following examples (where *C* stands for consonant and *V* for vowel):

One consonant—CV *see*
Two consonants—CCV *blue*
Three consonants—CCCV *screw*

Furthermore, English can have up to three consonants in word-final position:

One consonant—VC *up*
Two consonants—VCC *ask*
Three consonants—VCCC *asks*

Phonotactic rules vary from language to language. In Japanese and Hawaiian, for instance, consonant clusters are phonotactically impossible. The syllable pattern predominant in these languages is consonant-vowel (CV). The Japanese words *sushi*, *kimono*, and *sumo* and the Hawaiian *Honolulu* illustrate this pattern.

When a language borrows a word from another language, the sound structure of the loan word is adjusted to fit the phonotactics of the borrower. Consider, for instance, how Japanese has naturalized borrowed English words. The Japanese word derived from the English *girlfriend* is pronounced 'gurufurendu'; the word *sunglasses* in Japanese is pronounced "sunugurasu."

Because Japanese is so different from English phonotactically, Japanese learners of English will often insert additional vowels into English consonant clusters. For instance, a Japanese ESL student may pronounce the word *street* "suturito" and realize the word *screw* as "sukuru," inserting additional vowels between the consonants.

This phenomenon of sound insertion is called *epenthesis*. You can observe epenthesis in the speech of Spanish learners of English when they produce "espeak" and "estreet" for *speak* and *street*, respectively. In these cases, epenthesis is brought about by the Spanish phonotactic rule that does not allow word-initial sound clusters beginning with [s].

Consider an example of another phonotactic rule, this time from Italian. Because, in Italian, words tend to end with vowel sounds (e.g., *Roma*, *Milano*), Italian language learners epenthesize final English consonants, for instance, pronouncing *big* as "biguh."

Some language learners may practice *deletion*, or leaving out sounds in consonant clusters. For instance, because Cantonese and Vietnamese languages lack consonant clusters, speakers of these languages may delete one or both sounds from an English consonant cluster. Thus, *green* may be realized as "geen" and *past* pronounced "pat" or even "pa."

On first glance, a speaker of English may find it surprising that simple English words such as *street* or *student* present pronunciation challenges. In order to put yourself in the language learner's shoes, try to pronounce words from languages that manifest phonotactic patterns not found in English. Try, for instance, saying *mts'vrtneli* ("trainer") in Georgian, a Caucasian language spoken in the Republic of Georgia.

Stress and Rhythm

You may have heard people pass judgment on the way a foreign language sounds. For instance, speakers of English may perceive Spanish as being spoken "too rapidly" or German as sounding "too harsh." It goes without saying that no language is inherently superior to another one, and that pronouncements of this sort reflect people's arbitrary preferences and occasional prejudices. Still, it is important to bear in mind that perceptions of pronunciation are based on some reality, since not only the sounds but also the stress and rhythm patterns of different languages are quite distinct. We now say a few words about these distinctions.

Let us begin with stress. *Stress* (or accent) is prominence assigned to a syllable. A stressed syllable is louder, longer, and higher-pitched than those that are unstressed. Of all the world's languages, English word stress is probably heaviest, with the exception of German, its close relative. Figure 2.2 demonstrates the relative weight carried by stressed syllables in English and French.

You can see that, in English, the stressed syllable is pronounced with a much greater outlay of energy than the unstressed ones. In contrast, in French, the prominence of stressed and unstressed syllables is about the same.

Because so much energy goes into pronouncing stressed English vowels, the unstressed ones are affected by vowel reduction. They are often realized as *schwas*. The schwa is a mid-central vowel of indefinite quality, like the initial vowel in the word *above*.

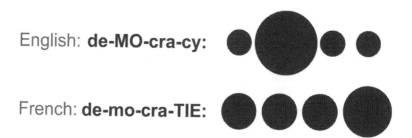

English: **de-MO-cra-cy:**

French: **de-mo-cra-TIE:**

Figure 2.2   Word stress in English and French.

An experiment demonstrates the reduction of the full vowel form to a schwa. Paying attention to the underlined vowels, say the following word pairs:

_CA_nada	_Ca_NA_dian_
de_MO_cracy	demo_CR_atic

Note the difference in the pronunciation of the same syllable, depending on whether it is stressed or unstressed. In both cases, the unstressed syllable is pronounced with a schwa.

While schwas are very common in English (indeed, about 30% of all English vowels are realized as schwas!), these vowels are often mispronounced by language learners. Speakers of languages that do not manifest vowel reduction may realize *campus* as 'campoos' and *difficult* as "difficoolt."

English stress is not only heavier than the stress of most languages; it is also distinct in that it is variable and can fall on virtually any syllable. Consider some examples:

First syllable stressed:	*REalize*
	HOrrible
	CIrculate
Second syllable stressed:	*inSIpid*
	couRAgeous
	eROsion
Third syllable stressed:	*interRUPT*
	obsoLETE
	represent

Mastering variable English stress may present challenges to those students who speak languages with a fixed stress, such as, for instance, French or Spanish, both of which, to simplify matters considerably, tend to have stress on the final syllable. Cognates, or similar-sounding words, may be particularly problematic, causing students to realize *DIfficult* as *diffiCULT* and *TOtal* as *toTAL*.

Let us now talk about sentence stress, or pronouncing some words with extra prominence in connected speech. It can be said that, in English, sentence stress parallels syllable stress. While some words in a sentence are pronounced with great prominence, others are contracted. The stressed words are the so-called content words (e.g., nouns, verbs, adjectives, question words); the unstressed words are function words (e.g., auxiliaries, prepositions, articles). English speakers pronounce unstressed words indistinctly, with schwas and also with deleted final and initial consonants. For instance, *from* is reduced to "frm," *his* realized as "iz," *and* as "n," and so on. In connected speech, the sentence *His wife and his children just came from Paris* may be pronounced "Iz wife 'n 'iz children js' came frm Paris." Note that these sound reductions and deletions are by no means incorrect or sloppy, and they are used by speakers of various educational backgrounds.

The alternation of stressed and unstressed words in English follows a pattern. Content words come out rhythmically, within equal time intervals, irrespective of the number of the intervening function words.

Consider Figure 2.3. Even though sentences 2 and 3 contain more words than sentence 1, pronouncing the three sentences takes about the same time, because each one has the same number of stressed words. English and other Germanic languages (e.g., Dutch and German) in which stressed words are delivered rhythmically are called *stress-timed*.

Let us perform an experiment to see how stress timing works. Start beating rhythmically on the table while saying the first sentence in Figure 2.3. Keep saying *Trees need water*, making sure that each stressed word is pronounced with one beat. Once you have established a steady beating rhythm, say sentences 2 and 3. If you are a native speaker of English, you should say all three sentences within three beats.

In contrast to stress-timed languages, in *syllable-timed* languages (e.g., Greek, Hindi, Spanish, Turkish), *all* syllables (whether they be stressed or unstressed), come out rhythmically in connected speech. It is because of the constant syllable beat of these languages that English speakers may perceive them as being unrelentingly rapid.

It is sometimes said that stress-timed languages have a "Morse-code rhythm," while syllable-timed languages have a "machine-gun" rhythm.

1.	TREES		NEED		WATER.
2. The	TREES	might	NEED	some	WATER.
3. The	TREES	might've	NEEDED	some	WATER.

Figure 2.3   Rhythmical pronunciation of stressed syllables in English.

Implications for Instruction

1. Understanding where and how a sound is articulated helps language learners develop target-like pronunciation. Design mini-lessons that explicitly discuss the place and manner of articulation of the English consonants [ɹ], [θ], and [ð].

2. Greek-speaking students of English may realize *sure* as "sewer," and Korean-speaking students pronounce *finish* as "pinish." You may recall that the absence of a sound from the student's home language is a frequent source of errors. Based on the examples above, what can you say about the sound systems of Greek and Korean?

3. Here is a scenario of a pronunciation lesson gone wrong. The teacher repeatedly demonstrates a pair of similar sounds (e.g., "rrrr" and "llll"). However, the students still fail to perceive the difference between the two. The thing is that students have difficulty distinguishing between pairs of sounds when these are taught in isolation. Pronunciation lessons are infinitely more effective when students are taught to distinguish between words (e.g., *light/right*), instead of just individual sounds. Design a mini-lesson that presents the [l] and [ɹ] sounds within the context of minimal pairs.

4. While English word stress is variable, it is by no means random. Conduct a study to research the patterns of English word stress. Design engaging activities with a focus on word stress.

WORDS TO REMEMBER

phonetics: the study of speech sounds and how they are produced and perceived.

phonology: the study of speech sounds as a system and speakers' knowledge of that system.

initiation: creating the airstream needed for speech-sound production.

articulation: shaping the airstream involved in speech-sound production.

consonants: speech sounds created with some obstruction of the airstream.

vowels: speech sounds created with no obstruction of the airstream.

vocal cords: two bands of muscles stretched horizontally across the larynx.

voiced speech sounds: speech sounds accompanied by vibration of the vocal cords.

voiceless speech sounds: speech sounds produced without vibration of the vocal cords.

bilabials: consonants articulated with both lips.

labiodentals: consonants articulated with the lower lip and upper teeth.

alveolar consonants: consonants articulated with the tongue tip against the alveolar ridge.

retroflex consonants: consonants articulated with the tongue curled backward.

palatals: consonants articulated with the back of the tongue against the palate.

velars: consonants articulated with the back of the tongue against the soft palate.

glottals: consonants articulated with narrowing of the glottis.

stops: consonants articulated with full obstruction of the airstream.

fricatives: consonants articulated with partial obstruction of the airstream.

affricates: consonants initiated as stops and released as fricatives.

approximants: consonants articulated with minimal obstruction of the airstream.

tense vowels: vowels articulated with the tense tongue muscles.

lax vowels: vowels articulated with the lax tongue muscles.

diphthong: a vowel characterized by an audible change in sound quality.

glide: the final trailing element of diphthongs.

phoneme: a sound that distinguishes one word from another.

allophone: a variant of a phoneme that does not change meaning.

tone: in tone languages, pitch patterns that distinguish words.

phonotactics: language-specific rules for combining speech sounds.

epenthesis: insertion of an extra sound.

deletion: leaving out a sound.

schwa: a central mid vowel commonly pronounced in unstressed syllables in NAE.

stress-timed language: a language whose stressed syllables occur rhythmically.

syllable-timed language: a language in which all syllables occur rhythmically.

3

Grammar

Morphology

This chapter deals with grammar, or language rules. We start with a discussion of *morphology*, the linguistic discipline that deals with word-level grammar. The term "morphology" is derived from the Greek words *morphe*, meaning "form," and *logos*, meaning "study." Morphological studies investigate word form; they research the building blocks of words and describe how these are pieced together.

Let us consider some of these building blocks. Take the word *unlikely*. It can be broken down into three parts: *un-*, *-like-*, and *-ly*. Each of these pieces carries some meaning of its own. For instance, *un-* expresses negation, *-like-* means "possible," and *-ly* suggests the manner in which an action is performed. Or take another word, *ducklings*. This word has three elements: *duck-* denotes a genus of waterfowl, *-ling* refers to this animal's young, and *-s* signifies plurality. All of the word elements listed here are *morphemes*. They are the smallest language elements that carry meaning.

Why is a morpheme described as being the "smallest" meaningful language element? The reason is that, while we can indeed split morphemes such as *un-* or *mark* into even smaller pieces, such as *n* or *m*, these sounds

The Educator's Guide to Linguistics, pages 33–48
Copyright © 2012 by Information Age Publishing
All rights of reproduction in any form reserved.

are void of any meaning of their own. In other words, it is impossible to break up a morpheme without "spilling" meaning.

But what about *a* or *s*, you might ask? Are these small pieces of language phonemes or morphemes? The answer is both—or, rather—it depends. While the *a* that occurs in the word *cat* is a phoneme, the *a-* in the word *apolitical* is a morpheme of negation. Similarly, while *s* is a phoneme in *so*, it is a morpheme meaning "more than one" in the words *hats* and *cats*.

Based on their form, morphemes are divided into two groups: *free morphemes* and *bound morphemes*. Morphemes are said to be "free" when they can occur alone without being attached to other morphemes. Some examples of English free morphemes are the stems *a, shall, cat, hit,* or *stand.* Unlike free morphemes, bound morphemes cannot stand alone; they are always attached to other morphemes. Some examples of English bound morphemes are suffixes, prefixes, and endings such as *un-, re-, de-, -ful, -ly,* and *-s.*

Depending on the role they play in the language system, free morphemes are further divided into two subgroups: lexical and functional morphemes. While lexical morphemes are content words (e.g., *cat, small, catch*), functional morphemes are grammar words (e.g., *the, in, after*).

Bound morphemes also play two kinds of roles and are similarly divided into two subclasses: derivational and inflectional morphemes. Whereas derivational morphemes (e.g., *-er, un-, re-*) are used for creating new words out of already existing ones (e.g., *fight–fighter, interesting–uninteresting, cycle–recycle*), inflectional morphemes change the grammatical form of words without changing their underlying meaning. For instance, inflectional morphemes make nouns plural (e.g., *book–books*) or form the past tense of verbs (e.g., *kick–kicked*). Table 3.1 shows two different classes and four subclasses of morphemes. The "Functions" column on the right provides clues to help you understand how morphemes are classified.

Parts of Table 3.1 are shaded because the morphemes in the shaded boxes have something in common. The functional, derivational, and inflectional morphemes make up the so-called *closed class.* This class is called

TABLE 3.1 Types of Morphemes

Classes	Subclasses	Functions
Free morphemes	Lexical morphemes (e.g., *cook, make, taste, stove*)	Content words
	Functional morphemes (e.g., *will, in*)	Grammar words
Bound morphemes	Derivational morphemes (e.g., *-er, un-*)	Word creators
	Inflectional morphemes (e.g., *-s, -ed*)	Form changers

"closed" because the number of morphemes it contains is very small and extremely unlikely to expand. In contrast, lexical morphemes belong to the *open class* of morphemes. This category is huge and ever evolving, with new entries being coined every minute. While open-class morphemes can be compared to the ever-replenished building material of language, closed-class morphemes are like an efficient toolkit for assembling words and sentences out of that building material.

In English, bound morphemes are usually placed at the end of a word, in final position (e.g., *helps*). This tendency to place bound morphemes last is found not only in English, but also in other languages. Consider an example from Nahuatl (pronounced "nah-wahtl"). Popularly known as Aztecan, Nahuatl was once the language of the formidable Aztec empire and continues to be used to this day, mostly in rural Mexico. Nahuatl nouns end with the suffix *-tl*. This same suffix is found in the name of the language itself: *Nahuatl*. The following familiar words—which were borrowed, by the way, into English via Spanish—are examples of Nahuatl nouns featuring this suffix:

xocolātl ("chocolate")
coyōtl ("coyote")
tomatl ("tomato")

Placing the bound morpheme last makes sense. Given that the content information provided by the lexical morpheme is more important for communication than the relational information provided by the bound morpheme, it stands to reason that the latter should be moved to the end of the word. While placing the bound morpheme first, in initial position (e.g., *dislike*), is significantly less common, it is also possible.[1]

In Arabic, for instance, the definite article *al-* is a bound morpheme that gets attached to the front of a word. This attached article can be observed in some Arabic words that have been borrowed into English (e.g., *algebra, alcohol, alchemy*). The bound-morpheme-first order is also found in Swahili, where the prefix *m-*, which signifies human beings, can be seen in the words *mtu* ("person") and *mtoto* ("child").

Generally, there are more differences than similarities between the morphological systems of the world's languages. Let us now explore these differences in more detail to understand exactly how different languages put their morphological toolkits to work.

Fusion

We start our discussion with the English bound morpheme *-s*. This short morpheme is supposed to be attached to the verb in sentences such as *He reads*, *She likes*, or *It stands*; however, it is sometimes left out, to the chagrin of language teachers. The verb ending *-s* is a heavy lifter. It performs three jobs, or has three meanings, at the same time. Thus, it denotes the third person, the singular number, and the present tense of the verb.

The process of combining several grammatical meanings in a single bound morpheme is called *fusion*. To understand the morphological process of fusion a little better, it might be helpful to compare it to smelting. Not only does fusion blend together several grammatical meanings, it often attaches a bound morpheme to the stem with such force that the stem and the bound morpheme interpenetrate, with the stem becoming altered in the process. Consider the English bound morpheme *-th*. When *-th* is attached to the adjective stem, the former becomes transformed—as may be seen in the word pairs *long–length* and *broad–breadth*.

While fusion is rare in English, some languages, known as *fusional languages*, make extensive use of this morphological process. Prototypical examples of this group include some Latin-based languages, such as Italian and Spanish, as well as Slavic languages, including Russian, Polish, Ukrainian, and Chekh. Let us examine an example of fusion in Spanish.

Here are some forms of the Spanish verb *tener* ("to have"):

yo tengo ("I have")
tú tienes ("you [singular] have")
usted/él/ella tiene ("he/she has")
nosotros/as tenemos ("we have")
vosotros/as tenéis ("you (plural) have")
ustedes/ellos/ellas tienen ("they have")

Agglutination

Another morphological process, known as *agglutination*, can be described as being the opposite of fusion. While fusion blends several meanings into one morpheme and then tightly "welds" the morpheme to the stem, agglutination uses one and only one unit of meaning for each separate morpheme and then rather loosely "glues" several of these morphemes together—thus giving rise to the name of the process. Languages that use agglutination, such as Japanese, Swahili, and Turkish, are called *agglutinative languages*.

Morphemes in agglutinative languages can be compared to strings of beads. There is usually the main bead—that is, the stem—followed by smaller beads, that is, bound morphemes that are strung to the stem. Because of this bead-like word structure, it is always easy to single out individual morphemes in agglutinative languages.

To get a sense of how agglutinative languages work, let us begin with the Japanese verb *yaki* ("to grill"). (You may be familiar with this word from the name of the cooking style *teriyaki*, literally meaning "gloss-grill.") Consider the sentence below, which contains the word *yaki*:

> *Tanaka-san-wa tofu-wo yaki-masu.*
> ["Mr. Tanaka grills tofu." (Literally: "Mr. Tanaka tofu grills.")]

Note that each word in the sentence has a bound morpheme "glued" onto it. Thus, the *-wa* after Mr. Tanaka's name signifies the subject; the *-wo* added to *tofu* signals the direct object; and, finally, the bound morpheme *-masu* added to the verb denotes the present tense.

But what if you needed to say, "Mr. Tanaka does *not* grill tofu"? In that case, you would need to "glue" or add the bound morpheme *-n* to the bound morpheme *-mase*. This yields the following sentence:

> *Tanaka-san-wa tofu-wo yaki-mase-n.*
> ["Mr. Tanaka tofu grills not."]

And what if you wanted to use the past tense? In that case, you would need to add yet another agglutinative suffix. This time, it would be the suffix *deshita*. Accordingly, the Japanese for "Mr. Tanaka did not fry tofu" is:

> *Tanaka-san-wa tofu-wo yaki-mase-n-deshita.*
> ["Mr. Tanaka tofu grills not PAST TENSE."]

How about questions in Japanese? You have probably guessed that an agglutinative suffix needs to be added to the verb. In this case, that would be the question suffix *-ka*. Thus, the question 'Didn't Mr. Tanaka fry tofu?' takes the following form:

> *Tanaka-san-wa tofu-wo yaki-mase-n-deshita-ka?*
> ["Mr. Tanaka tofu grills not PAST TENSE QUESTION."]

As you can see, in agglutinative languages, increasingly complex grammatical meanings can be expressed by adding more and more morphemes. Agglutinative languages are distinct in that they have a large number of bound morphemes per stem. In effect, words in agglutinative languages can be very long. Here is an example of an unlikely but possible word in Turkish:

> *çekoslovakyalılaştıramayacaklarımızdan mıydınız?*
> ["Were you one of those whom we are not going to be able to turn into Czechoslovakians?"][2]

Isolating Languages

Do all languages use prefixes, suffixes, and endings to change grammatical form and coin new words out of those that already exist? The answer is no. Surprising as it may seem to speakers of fusional and agglutinative languages, there are languages that have very few bound morphemes or none whatsoever. These languages have neither markers of plurality, like the English -*s*, nor past-tense markers, like the English -*ed*.

The languages that make limited or no use of bound morphemes are called *isolating languages.* Chinese, Vietnamese, and Samoan are typical examples. But how do speakers of, say, Chinese make a distinction between one thing and many things, one person and many persons? How do they express the past tense? In cases where fusional or agglutinative languages use bound morphemes, Chinese uses words, such as numerals or nouns. Similarly, Chinese does not mark time with bound morphemes, but rather with certain time words. For instance, future action is often implied by such words as *yào* ("want"), or *míngtiān* ("tomorrow"). In a situation where an English speaker says, "I will go to see a movie tomorrow," a Chinese speaker says,

> *Míngtiān wǒ qù kàn diànyǐng.*
> ["Tomorrow I go look movie."]

or

> *Wǒ yào qù kàn diànyǐng.*
> ["I want go look movie."][3]

But what mechanism do isolating languages use to create new words? In English we often use derivational morphemes for this purpose. For instance, to create names for new instruments and gadgets, English often makes use of Latin stems that take the suffixes -er or -or. Thus, the device for transferring electrical energy is called a *transformer*, and that for producing energy is called a *generator*.

To create new words, Chinese, an isolating language, void of bound morphemes, relies extensively on *compounding*, that is, joining lexical morphemes together. The short Chinese words make for excellent "compounding material." Thus, when a name for a new technological invention is needed, short words meaning "engine," "machine," or "implement" are added to another stem. Here are some Chinese names of technological devices and their literal translations:

> transformer: *biànyāì*—literally, [change electric pressure implement]
> generator: *fādiànjī*—literally, [emit electricity engine]
> telephone: *diànhuà*—literally, [electric speech]
> computer: *diànnǎo*—literally, [electric brain]

Using compounding, rather than derivational morphemes, to coin names for science terms can offer certain advantages to speakers of Chinese. Unless you know a little Latin, you likely do not have a clear idea as to what the words *transformer* and *generator* actually mean. In contrast, because Chinese technological and scientific terms are morphologically transparent, it is easier to grasp their meaning. For instance, you would probably have no difficulty guessing that *fēijī*, or "fly engine," is the Chinese word for "airplane."

To appreciate how pervasive compounding is in Chinese, consider several English loan words of Chinese origin. Note that all of these words are compounds!

> *feng shui*—literally, [wind water]
> *kowtow*—literally, [bump head]
> *lo mein*—literally, [scoop noodle]
> *shar pei*—literally, [sand skin]
> *tycoon*—literally, [great nobleman]
> *typhoon*—literally, [great wind]

Incorporation

Now you know that, because isolating languages lack bound morphemes, they rely on compounding for word formation. Of course, Chinese is not the only language that uses this word-formation process. English, too, has numerous compound words, such as *armrest, campfire, bedbug,* and many, many others. But neither English nor even Chinese use compounding nearly as consistently as do the so-called *incorporating languages.*

Languages in the Eskimo-Aleut family, as well as the Chuckchi-Kamchatkan languages of the native population of Siberia, are called "incorporating" because they use a unique type of compounding whereby the verb incorporates its object. While compound verbs such as *stirfry* or *slamdunk* do exist in English, most English compounds are nouns. In incorporating languages, however, there are numerous compound verbs. In these languages, you may find verbs that mean something like "paddle-boated" or "down-streamed" or even "paddle-boated-quickly-and-then-down-streamed-with-his-wife."

Incorporating languages are unique in that their verbs can be really, really long. Verbs in these languages can incorporate two, three, four, or even more verb stems, as well as object modifiers such as adverbs and adjectives. Even more intriguingly, incorporating languages are distinct in that the verb can include not only objects but even a subject. As a result, the difference between a word and a sentence in these languages at times becomes blurred, as in the Eskimo sentence-word below:

> "Also he can probably make big boats"
> *Angyar-pa-li-yugnga-yugnar-quq-llu*
> boat + big + make + be able + probably + third-person singular + also[4]

Transfix Languages

In the beginning of this chapter, we discussed that bound morphemes in fusional and agglutinative languages are more commonly attached to the word's end than to its beginning. It is important to bear in mind, however, that bound morphemes do not only occur at the beginnings or ends of words. In Semitic languages, such as Arabic or Hebrew, bound morphemes are injected right into the body of the stem. These bound morphemes are called *transfixes.* Let us see how transfixes work.

Arabic and Hebrew roots are different from stems in, say, English, in that they have no vowels and are just made of consonants. There are roots of two, three, and four consonants. For instance, in both Arabic and Hebrew, the triconsonantal root SLM means "peace." (The SLM root is found in the Arabic and Hebrew greetings *Salam-aleikum!* and *Shalom!*, respectively.)

Transfix languages make words and express grammatical meanings by inserting vowels between the consonants of consonantal roots. Below are some examples of Arabic words based on the triconsonantal root SLM:

SaLiMa—"be safe, well"
SaLaMa—"make peace with somebody, treat somebody peaceably"
iSLaM—"submission to God"

Here is another triconsonantal Arabic root: HRM, meaning "sacred." The root HRM is used in the following words with which you may be familiar:

HaRaM—"forbidden," "sacred"
HaReeM—"private space"
beir allah al HaRaM—"house of God sacred" (the name of the Kaaba building in Saudi Arabia)

To understand transfixes a little better, it may be helpful to draw an analogy with construction. Semitic-language roots of two, three, and four consonants can be compared to two-, three-, and four-pronged carcasses. Each consonant or "carcass" expresses some basic concept. But it is only when speakers "pour" different vowel material into that carcass that the job of creating grammatical forms or new words is complete.

Syntax

While morphology deals with word-level grammar, syntax is the linguistic discipline concerned with sentence-level grammar. The word *syntax* is derived from the Greek word *syntaxis*, meaning "arrangement." Syntactic studies investigate word order and ways of joining words in a sentence.

The three building blocks of a sentence—the subject (S), the verb (V), and the object (O)—can be arranged in six possible ways: SVO, SOV, VSO, VOS, OSV, and OVS. Table 3.2 reveals the frequency of these syntactic patterns among the world's languages.

As you can see, the SVO and SOV word orders are the most common ones. For instance, the SVO (*I like coffee*) word order is predominant in English. The SOV word order is typical of Japanese and Korean. It can be found in the Japanese sentence we examined earlier: *Tanaka-san-wa tofu-wo yaki-masu* [literally: "Mr. Tanaka tofu grills"].

The VSO word order was used in Classical Arabic and can still be found in Modern Standard Arabic. An example of the VSO word order can be

TABLE 3.2   Distribution of the Six Basic Word Orders[5]

Word order	%	Languages
I like coffee. SVO	45%	English, French, German, Swahili, and many others
I coffee like. SOV	40%	Japanese, Korean, Hindi, Tamil, Persian, and many others
Like I coffee. VSO	10%	Classical Arabic, Hawaiian, and a few others
Like coffee I. VOS	3%	Fijian and Malagasy and a few others
Coffee I like. OSV	1%	Xavante (a native language spoken in Brazil) and Warao (a native language spoken in Venezuela)
Coffee like I. OVS	1%	Hixkaryana (an extinct native language once spoken in Brazil)

observed in the Arabic phrase *In šā Allāh* (pronounced "in shah alah"), which, translated word for word, means "if wills God." When a speaker of Arabic is describing her plans for the future, her interlocutor is likely to exclaim, *In šā Allāh!*, or "God willing!" (By the way, the Spanish *ojalá* and the Portuguese *oxalá*, both meaning "hopefully," are derived from this Arabic phrase.) For the purposes of our discussion, it is important to emphasize that in the phrase *In šā Allāh!* the verb, *šā*, comes before the subject, *Allāh*.

The OSV and OVS word orders are extremely rare, but, remarkably enough, they too can be found—mostly in the languages spoken in the Amazon basin.

Now you know that word order varies from language to language. But there is yet another important way in which languages differ from each other. While in some languages a particular word order is predominant, other languages are much more flexible about how they arrange words in a sentence. Linguists describe these two types of languages as having *fixed word order* and *free word order*.

Why is it that word order in some languages is fixed, while in others it is free? To answer this question, let us first consider another one: How do you know which word is the subject and which the object in an English sentence? The answer is simple: by its place in the sentence. Thus, the English subject tends to be in sentence-initial position, and the object follows the verb:

I   like   coffee
S   V   O

In contrast to English, other languages, such as Russian and Latin, rely on a rich system of bound morphemes to show whether a given word is the subject or the object of a sentence. Because their bound morphemes already convey this important grammatical information, speakers of free-word-order languages are at liberty to move their words around. For example, in the Russian sentence "Mikhail loves Moscow" (*Mikhail lyubit Moskvu.*), the name of the capital, *Moskva*, changes to *Moskvu*. It is the morpheme *-u* that signals that the name of the Russian capital is the object of the sentence, making free word order a possibility. Thus, speakers of Russian can say

1. ["Mikhail loves Moscow."] SVO—*Mikhail lyubit Moskvu.*
2. ["Mikhail Moscow loves."] SOV—*Mikhail Moskvu lyubit.*
3. ["Loves Mikhail Moscow."] VSO—*Lyubit Mikhail Moskvu.*
4. ["Loves Moscow Mikhail."] VOS—*Lyubit Moskvu Mikhail.*
5. ["Moscow Mikhail loves."] OSV—*Moskvu Mikhail lyubit.*
6. ["Moscow loves Mikhail."] OVS—*Moskvu lyubit Mikhail.*

The Russian sentences above all have slightly different emphases. What is important, though, is that they are all possible and that they all share the same basic meaning.

Now, let us look into different ways of linking words together in a sentence. Consider the English sentence *I see him*. The pronoun form *him* is used here (not *he*!) because such is the "ruling" of the verb *see*, which "dictates" that the form of the pronoun be changed from *he* to *him*. The pattern of joining words together whereby a word dictates the grammatical form of the adjacent word is called *government*.

Let us consider another example of government. The Latin for "day" is *dies*. However, in the Latin phrase *Carpe diem!* (or "Seize the day!"), the noun form is changed from *dies* to *diem*. It is the verb *carpe* that is responsible for the form change.

There exists a more "egalitarian" mechanism of joining words together. This syntactic mechanism is called *agreement*. In instances of agreement, two words "agree" or correspond to each other in terms of their grammatical form.

In English, the form of the verb *to be* agrees with the form of the adjacent pronoun both in person and in number: *I am, you are, he or she is, we are, you are, they are*. Here, the two words in each pair have the same grammatical form; *I*, for instance, is in the first-person singular, and so is *am*. Now consider another example. In French, nouns fall into two classes: the feminine and the masculine gender.[6] Because, in French, adjectives as well as articles must agree with the noun grammatically, French uses different forms of articles and adjectives, depending on whether the noun is masculine or feminine. For instance, because the name of the country *France* is feminine, the feminine forms of the article and adjective are used in the phrase *la belle France,* meaning "the beautiful France." In contrast, because the word for "world," *monde,* is masculine, the masculine article and adjective are used with this noun, which is why the French for "beautiful world" or "high society" is *le beau monde.*

Some languages have particularly rich patterns of agreement. In Swahili, for instance, there are 16 genders or classes of nouns. There are separate genders for persons, trees, natural forces, artifacts, and abstract nouns, among others. Swahili nouns of different genders must agree with the words they are attached to. For instance, because nouns in the person category start with the bound morpheme *m-* (e.g., *mtoto* ["child"]), the words that go with them must take *m-,* too. Similarly, because artifact nouns start with the bound morpheme *ki-* (e.g., *kitabu* ["book"]), the words that go with them must also start with that prefix. Here are some examples:

> *mtoto mmoja*
> ["child one"]
> "one child"
> *kitabu kimoja*
> ["book one"]
> "one book"{

Descriptive and Prescriptive Grammars

This chapter provides just a miniscule sampling of the rules that describe morphological and syntactic patterns in different languages. These rules, as you have undoubtedly noticed, are extremely complex. In fact, there is no such thing as a grammatically simple language. A huge tome is needed to cover even the basic morphosyntactic patterns of any language, and linguists spend years writing these rules down. The extensive treatises that result from these endeavors are called *descriptive grammars.* A descriptive grammar is a collection of rules that describe (hence the word "descriptive') the entire set of sentences that may be produced by native speakers of a given language.

Native speakers do not consciously know the descriptive grammars of their own languages. To be sure, a native speaker would notice that there is something wrong with the sentence *I see he.* (The asterisk * here indicates that this sentence is impossible or malformed.) And yet, while native speakers would be able to fix the broken sentence, they would be hard pressed to explain which rules dictate the use of *him* rather than *he.*

Aside from descriptive grammars, there exist much more succinct grammars, of which most educated speakers have conscious knowledge. These so-called *prescriptive grammars* prescribe (hence the word "prescriptive") the language norms of a given language. Prescriptive grammars lay down the rules of proper language use—those that well-educated speakers are expected to follow. For instance, according to a prescriptive rule of English grammar, one is supposed to say, *My friend and I*, not *Me and my friend*. From the viewpoint of descriptive grammar, there is nothing wrong with either sentence: both occur in the speech of native speakers. Prescriptive grammar, however, rejects the second one.

Prescriptive grammars tend to be written when speakers of a language come to the realization that they are part of a nation and become proud of their language. At that moment in the nation's history, the language is *codified* or standardized

Many prescriptive rules of English grammar were written in the 18th century by a linguist named Robert Lowth. Lowth admired Latin, believed that it was an ideal, supremely "logical" language, and aspired to impose the rules of Latin grammar on English. For instance, on the grounds that in Latin it is impossible to end a sentence with a preposition, Lowth posited a similar rule for English, dictating that sentences such as *That's what we are interested in* should be banished, at least from written speech. Similarly, Lowth found *double negation* (as in *I don't know nothing*) objectionable because this pattern was not found in Latin texts. These, as well as many other rules of prescriptive grammar, are rather artificial and not always easy to follow. For instance, it is impossible to avoid putting the preposition at the end of the sentence *She is sought after*. According to one story (probably apocryphal), Winston Churchill poked fun at this rule when he quipped, "This is the kind of tedious nonsense up with which I will not put."

Linguists never tire of reminding us that the rules of prescriptive grammar are not God given. Rather, they are arbitrary and reflect the beliefs and prejudices of the writer. That said, in spite of linguists' efforts to provide a more objective perspective on prescriptive grammars, most speakers revere prescriptive norms, feel protective of them, and are irked when they are violated.

Implications for Instruction

1. Each language uses its morphological toolkit to integrate borrowed words into its fabric. It is particularly illuminating to watch these morphological processes in immigrant communities, where

new words are borrowed on a very large scale into the speaker's home language. Consider the following examples:

marketa ("market") (used by Spanish-speaking immigrants in English-speaking countries)

ocAshit' ("to cash") (used by Russian-speaking immigrants in English-speaking countries)

Can you identify Spanish and Russian bound morphemes in the words above?

2. Chinese learners of English produce phrases such as **I have two book* or **Last year I work*. How can you account for these errors in light of what you know about Chinese morphology?

3. Divergence in the syntactic patterns of languages is responsible for the patterns of errors made by English-language learners. Given that English-language learners from Korea produce sentences such as **I ice-cream like* and **I book read*, what can you say about word order in Korean?

4. In light of what you know about the use of agreement in French, explain the two forms of the word *new* in the French expressions *nouvelle cuisine* ("new cuisine") and *nouveau riche* ("the new rich").

5. Utterances such as *Me and my friend* and *With who?* are produced by native speakers. However, they are incorrect from the viewpoint of prescriptive grammar, which dictates that the proper forms are *My friend and I* and *With whom?* Do you think it is important to teach these and other prescriptive grammar rules when so often they are not observed by native speakers?

WORDS TO REMEMBER

morphology: word-level grammar.

syntax: sentence-level grammar.

morpheme: the minimal unit of language that carries meaning.

free morphemes: morphemes that can stand alone (e.g., *cat, dog, the, in*).

bound morphemes: morphemes that are attached to other morphemes (e.g., *un-, -ing*).

lexical morphemes: content words (e.g., *big, house*).

functional morphemes: grammar words, such as auxiliaries, prepositions, and articles.

derivational morphemes: morphemes used to create new words (e.g., *un-*, *-er*).

inflectional morphemes: morphemes used to change word forms (e.g., *-s*, *-ed*)

closed class of morphemes: the limited and unchanging set of functional, derivational, and inflectional morphemes.

open class of morphemes: the ever-expanding set of lexical morphemes.

fusion: a morphological process whereby a single bound morpheme that combines several meanings is attached to a stem.

agglutination: a morphological process whereby several bound morphemes, each carrying only one unit of meaning, are attached to a stem.

isolating languages: languages that lack bound morphemes and express relational information with the help of content words.

incorporation: a morphological process of compounding several lexical morphemes within a verb.

transfix: a morphological process whereby vowel morphemes are inserted between the consonants of consonantal roots.

fixed word order: inflexible word order, mostly found in languages lacking in bound morphemes.

free word order: flexible word order, mostly found in languages with well-developed systems of bound morphemes.

government: a way of linking words such that one word dictates the form of another one.

agreement: a way of linking words in a sentence, in which words show a particular feature.

descriptive grammar: a system of rules outlining all the possible morphological and syntactic patterns of a given language.

prescriptive grammar: a system of rules laying down patterns of proper, well-educated language use.

double negative: using two negatives in one phrase.

Notes

1. See for discussion Whaley, L. (1997). *Introduction to typology: The unity and diversity of language.* Thousand Oaks, CA: Sage.

2. Adapted from Lieber, R. (2010). *Introducing morphology.* Cambridge, UK: Cambridge University Press, p.120.
3. Adapted from Lyovin, A. (1997). *An introduction to the languages of the world.* New York: Oxford University Press, pp. 134–135.
4. Adapted from Lyovin, A. (1997). *An introduction to the languages of the world.* New York: Oxford University Press, p. 18.
5. Adapted from Song, J. J. (2001). *Linguistic typology: Morphology and syntax.* Harlow, UK: Pearson.
6. Grammatical gender, by the way, is not to be confused with sex. It simply denotes a certain type of noun.

4

Semantics

The word *semantics* and its derivatives *semantic* and *semantically* refer to language meaning. When there is a connection between the meanings of two words (as in the case of synonyms), we say that these words are "semantically related." When several words—for instance, *cup, eat,* and *meal*—are linked thematically, we say that they belong to a certain "semantic field." If the meaning of a word is obvious, we say that it is "semantically transparent."

The word *semantics* sometimes crops up in day-to-day conversation, as when we say, "That's just semantics," to refer to unnecessary, hair-splitting arguments over correct wording. Even though this phrase is used disparagingly, the words *semantics, semantic,* and *semantically* are neutral scientific terms.

Semantic Triangle

Now let us talk about word meaning. We are going to start with a little experiment. Close your eyes and say the word *flower*. There is a vibration in

The Educator's Guide to Linguistics, pages 49–64
Copyright © 2012 by Information Age Publishing

your brain: you experience the mental image of a flower. The meaning of the word is that vibration, that image that arises in your mind when you use a word whose meaning you know, whether it be *flower*, *book*, or *Washington, DC*.

This mental vibration does not involve straightforward imagery. It is not a mental picture that you "see" with your mind's eye when you recall a person or a place. Rather, word meaning is the quintessential idea of what constitutes a flower, a book, or Washington, DC, to name just a few examples. Scientists have several names for this idea, calling it a "gestalt," a "schema," an "Idealized Cognitive Model," and a "lexical concept." In this book, we employ the term *lexical concept* and use it interchangeably with the word *meaning*.

Now let us discuss what word meaning is *not*. The actual flower that grows in your backyard is not the meaning of the word *flower*. That flower is the *referent* of the word, if you are using it to speak of a plant in your garden. Similarly, the book you are holding in your hands while reading this chapter could be the referent of the word *book*, and the big, noisy city on the Potomac is the referent of the word *Washington, DC*.

Linguists represent the relationship between referent, word, and lexical concept using a model called the *semantic triangle* (Figure 4.1). The symbol and the referent, shown at the bottom of the triangle, are both found in real life (one as an acoustic or a graphic entity, the other as something in the world). In contrast, word meaning, represented by the top of the triangle, only exists in people's minds.

Gestalt Theory of Meaning

Let us now discuss some psychological studies that made particularly insightful contributions to our understanding of the mind, the seat of meaning.

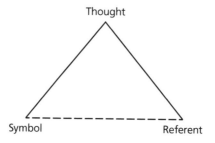

Figure 4.1 Semantic triangle.

In the 1920s, Max Wertheimer, a Czech-born psychologist, was research-ing cognition. One day, while taking a train ride, Wertheimer noticed—as if for the first time—that the lights he saw flashing past the train's window seemed to be a single light jumping back and forth! The sight mesmerized Wertheimer. He quickly disembarked from the train, rushed to a nearby store, and bought a stroboscope (a flipbook-like toy that shows moving im-ages). Wertheimer then observed how the individual images in the strobo-scope merged into something like a mini movie.

Wertheimer and his colleagues helped make sense of these and other similar mental phenomena. They argued that our mind has a way of deal-ing with disconnectedness. It integrates disparate pieces of information into a whole and imbues this whole with meaning. Psychologists call these whole, meaningful mental entities *gestalts*.

A little experiment can demonstrate the process of gestalt making. Look at Figure 4.2. Even though this image technically consists of disjoint-ed dots and lines, your mind interprets it as showing two superimposed triangles. Out of disjointed bits and pieces, your mind has created a mental entity that is whole and meaningful.

Gestalts have a defining characteristic. Each gestalt is *more than the sum of its parts*.

How can something be more than the sum of its parts? Let's consider an analogy from baking. A cake is made of several ingredients. When you mix them and place the dough in the oven, the heat works on the mixture to create a treat whose taste cannot be reduced to those original ingredi-ents. Our productive mind is a bit like an oven. Out of the ingredients of information, it "bakes" whole and meaningful gestalts.

Figure 4.2   An incomplete drawing used to demonstrate holistic perception.

Scientists who espouse the gestalt theory of meaning argue that lexical entities are gestalts. They are whole, indivisible, and more than the sum of their parts.

Prototype Effect

At one time or another, most of us have been uncertain about the meaning of a word. For instance, we might muse, *Is this person smart or just book smart?* or, *Is this performer beautiful or pretty?* At other times, however, we apply a label with certainty. On those occasions, we say, *This person is definitely smart* or, *That one is undeniably beautiful.* Clearly, words have typical and less typical referents. But what is the pattern that makes us perceive some referents as typical and others as not?

This question was studied in the 1970s at the University of California by psychologist Eleanor Rosch.[1] Rosch asked her subjects to grade members of categories such as birds, furniture, or clothes and say which ones were more typical. She discovered that respondents consistently thought of some examples of birds as more "birdy," some furniture as more "furniture-like," and some clothes as more "clothes-like." For instance, respondents said that, while the robin is a good example of a *bird*, the toucan and emu are not (see Figure 4.3). Similarly, socks are better examples of *clothing* than are

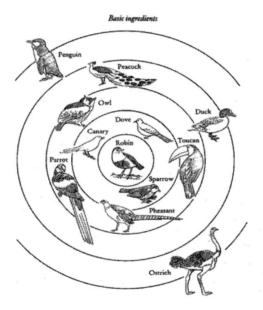

Figure 4.3   The less and more prototypical exemplars for the category *bird*. (Published with permission from Wiley and Sons).

aprons and earmuffs. Rosch also found that people took less time to recall some examples in a category. When asked to give an example of a *bird*, respondents were quick to name the robin and took more time to mention the toucan. Rosch called our tendency to perceive referents as being less and more typical the *prototype effect*. She called the typical, central example of a category its *prototype*.

Follow-up studies found that even seemingly unambiguous terms such as *even number* and *odd number*, *geometric figure*, and *female* are subject to the prototype effect. Thus, respondents indicated that they found 2 to be a more prototypical *even number* than 1,000, 3 a better example of an *odd number* than 501, a circle a more prototypical *geometric figure* than an ellipse, and a mother a more prototypical *female* than a comedienne.[2] People even have prototypes for abstract concepts. They feel, for instance, that there are typical and less typical examples of *lying*.

These findings suggest that lexical concepts have a specific configuration. While the central part of the concept, which is linked to the prototype, is "in focus," the periphery of the lexical concept is hazy. When we experience an entity, we check it against the prototype. If the entity matches our prototype, we use the word with confidence. Otherwise, we hesitate. Because of this notion of the hazy periphery of lexical concepts, linguists speak about the *fuzziness* of word meaning.

At first glance, this fuzziness would seem to render language inefficient. What kind of a semiotic system is language if we cannot even use word symbols with certainty? We may indeed run into misunderstandings or hesitate about applying words because of their semantic fuzziness. However, fuzziness has its merits. Because the periphery of word meaning is not clearly defined, we can stretch a concept and use an already existing word to name some other, less prototypical referent. It is due to the flexible properties of word meaning that the computer engineer who created a little oblong contraption with a cord extending from its body was able to name that particular gadget a *mouse*. Because of the fuzziness of word meaning, new words such as *keyboard, cut and paste, firewall*, and thousands of others have been created. An Internet firewall is not an actual wall, nor is a computer mouse an animal. However, as long as an object or an idea resembles another object or idea, we are happy to extend the name of one to the other.

Referring to an entity by the name of another entity because of a resemblance between the two is called *metaphor*. Metaphor is a highly productive mechanism of word formation.

Conceptual Metaphors

Sometimes, people invoke a certain comparison again and again. Consider the following expressions: *to have the <u>hots</u> for somebody; he is a <u>hottie</u>; to feel <u>warm</u> and fuzzy; to be <u>on fire</u>, <u>to ignite a passion</u>.* These phrases have something in common: they all compare affection to heat. Why is it that the comparison between love and heat has been made so many times?

This question has been researched by American scholars George Lakoff (pronounced "Lake-off") and Mark Johnson. Lakoff and Johnson came to the conclusion that metaphors are more than just stylistic devices. Instead, in their view, metaphorical expressions like the ones above are instruments of knowing. Whenever we want to wrap our minds around something complex and abstract, we liken it to something concrete. Lakoff and Johnson labeled these inquiry-oriented metaphorical expressions *conceptual metaphors* and found scores of them in our language.

For instance, they discovered that there are numerous conceptual metaphors based on the idea that LIFE IS A JOURNEY.[3] Consider the phrases below:

> *She is <u>on her way</u> to retirement.*
> *He <u>is headed</u> for disaster.*
> *Theirs was a <u>rocky</u> marriage.*
> *There is <u>light at the end of the tunnel</u>.*
> *We will <u>cross that bridge when we get there</u>.*
> *She is <u>at a crossroads</u>.*

Some bases for comparison are particularly productive. For instance, there exists a vast group of conceptual metaphors that make sense of abstraction in terms of the human body. Our upward orientation, our hands, and our eyes become the bases of such metaphors. Take the conceptual metaphor UP IS GOOD. The English language has scores of phrases that conceptualize the upward direction as something positive and the downward direction as something negative. Consider such contrasting words as *uplifting* and *depressing, cheer up* and *break down, feel high* and *feel low.*

Another group of body-related conceptual metaphors are based on the idea that RIGHT IS GOOD and LEFT IS BAD. Words and phrases such as *right on, righteous,* and *right-hand man,* on the one hand, and *out of left field* and *left-hand compliment,* on the other, illustrate our perception that things positioned on the right side of our body are positive, whereas things positioned on our left are negative. (Note that the RIGHT

IS GOOD and LEFT IS BAD metaphors have nothing to do with political orientation.)

Other body metaphors suggest that KNOWLEDGE IS SEEING and IGNORANCE IS NOT SEEING. When we speak about *being in the dark* or *enlightenment*, we are making a connection between our eyes and our cognition. Just think about the fact that, when we understand something, we say, *Oh, I see!*

If our bodies had been different, our conceptualization of the world would have been entirely different, too. What would our language have been like if, instead of being upright creatures who are pulled down by gravity and have pairs of hands and eyes, we were blind spheres suspended in weightlessness? It is impossible to say what kinds of words we would use, but we obviously would not have phrases like *he has two left feet, cheer up, it's really depressing, he is my right-hand man,* and *I see!*

Conceptual metaphors are thus rooted in our experiences. Let us now take a closer look at the connection between our words and our bodies. Recall the metaphor LOVE IS HEAT. We liken affection to heat because of the way we experience affection and arousal. The metaphor has a physiological basis.

While some conceptual metaphors are universal and physiologically determined, others are rooted in culture-specific beliefs and values. For instance, English has a number of conceptual metaphors that reflect the idea that TIME IS A VALUABLE THING. We say that we *waste time, save time, spend time,* and so on. These conceptual metaphors are rooted in the Western notion of time as a valuable commodity.

Whether conceptual metaphors are universal or culture-specific, they always compare something abstract to something concrete. Modern scholars argue that these comparisons reveal the workings of our minds: we know by means of metaphors.

There are some important points of difference between the conceptual metaphors and metaphors used as stylistic devices. First, poetic metaphors are used consciously. For instance, we can't help noticing the artistic effect of the metaphors when Shakespeare's Romeo exclaims, *"What light through yonder window breaks? / It is the east, and Juliet is the sun."* In contrast, we use conceptual metaphors unconsciously, without noticing the imagery behind them. When we say, *You are headed for disaster,* we don't think about someone traveling in the direction of a misfortune. Furthermore, poetic metaphors are one-of-a-kind creations. By comparing his beloved Juliet to the sun in the eastern sky, Shakespeare's Romeo made a statement without a precedent. In contrast, conceptual metaphors are not unique. People make some comparisons again and again, creating clusters of semantically related phrases.

The Linguistic Relativity Hypothesis

If you have studied a foreign language, you have undoubtedly noticed that different languages have very different grammars. You might also have noticed that certain concepts in English are not found in other languages, and vice versa.

The structural and semantic variety of languages is fascinating. Here is how Tom Reid, an American journalist who lived and worked in Japan, described the meaning of just one short Japanese word, *wa*, whose equivalent is not found in English:

> *Wa* is harmony—not musical, but social harmony. It is that mellow feeling that comes when people are getting along. It is working together in a state of mutual understanding. It is the absence of confrontation. For the Japanese in particular, and for the people of Asia in general, it is the preeminent social value [...]. The basic word *wa* is written with the character meaning "peace." In Japan, the idea is more commonly conveyed with the common word *chowa*, made from two characters that mean "a neat arrangement" and "peace." When the affairs of a family, or a neighborhood tea-ceremony society, or a classroom, company, or croquet club are neatly arranged so that all the members are getting along smoothly, that is a state of *chowa*.[4]

But what is the significance of the fact that languages do not match up semantically and structurally? Eighteenth-century German scholars believed that each language has a distinctive *Geist* or "spirit." The question was posed again in the 1920s by American linguist Edward Sapir and his student and fellow researcher Benjamin Whorf. Sapir, a linguistic anthropologist, studied Native American languages. He found that these languages had unique units of meaning that Western languages lacked. Together, Sapir and Whorf put forward the hypothesis that came to be known as the *Sapir–Whorf hypothesis*, or the *linguistic relativity hypothesis*. Sapir and Whorf believed that, because languages carve up reality in different ways, speakers of different languages are bound to have distinct worldviews. If a language does not have a word for a certain concept, its speakers cannot think in terms of this concept. As Sapir put it, people are "very much at the mercy of the particular language which has come to be the medium of expression for their society."[5]

Is there experimental proof of the linguistic relativity hypothesis? An important early study aimed at testing the hypothesis focused on the impact of color terms on the perception of color. Linguists have long known that color terms are vastly different across languages. Thus, English has 11 basic color terms: *white, black, red, green, yellow, blue, brown, purple, pink, orange,* and *gray*. In contrast, some New Guinea Highland languages only have words for "black" and "white"—or, rather, for something like "dark" and "light." Japanese *ao* can mean "green," "blue," or "pale," depending on the context (e.g., vegetables, the sea, clouds). Russian has two words for "blue": *goluboj*, meaning "baby blue," and *sinij*, meaning "navy blue."

Does the availability or absence of certain color terms have an impact on people's color perception? This question was explored by American linguists Brent Berlin and Paul Kay.[6] Using Munsell Color Chips, a color chart that portrays 300 colors, Berlin and Kay asked speakers to identify the best samples of various colors. They discovered that, even though color terms differ from language to language, the hues that respondents identified as being most typical fell within a very close range. Obviously, speakers of languages with fewer color terms could only be questioned about a narrower range of focal hues. The researchers' key finding, however, was that, irrespective of the number of color terms in their particular language, people recognized the same colors as being prototypical.

Berlin and Kay argued that the evidence they obtained had refuted the linguistic relativity hypothesis. Their finding that all people perceive similar hues as being typical is at odds with the linguistic relativity hypothesis because it demonstrates that words (or at least color terms) are not arbitrary labels. Rather, color terms grow out of people's physiology and are coined because of our natural predisposition to perceive reality in a certain way. According to this view, words are physiologically objective, not culturally subjective. This argues against thinking of language as taking people to a cognitive blind spot. Instead, it suggests that people use language to express their innate perception of the world.

Berlin and Kay's research, together with other similar evidence, seems to have debunked the linguistic relativity hypothesis. And yet, recent years have seen a revival of interest in Sapir and Whorf's ideas. Indeed, interest in this hypothesis seems to reappear whenever scientists discover a language with a particularly striking grammatical or semantic characteristic.

Consider Pirahã (pronounced "pee-dah-HAAN"), a language spoken by a tribe of hunter-gatherers who live under the rainforest canopy on the banks of the Maici River, a narrow, meandering tributary of the Amazon. Pirahã culture is unusual. Instead of sleeping through the night, Pirahã people take short naps throughout the day to replenish their energy. They have also been reported to go hungry for several days, not from lack of food, but rather in order to build endurance. The Pirahã language has a number of unusual characteristics. For instance, it has a voiceless trill, a sound of the kind you make when you blow air through your lips while vibrating them. The language of the Pirahã is also distinct in that it only has three counting words: *one, two,* and *many.*

Peter Gordon, one of the linguists interested in testing the linguistic relativity hypothesis, wondered if this limited arsenal of number words had an impact on numeracy cognition in the Pirahã. Gordon placed sets of objects, such as AAA batteries or nuts, in front of his respondents and asked them to assemble matching number sets. He discovered that his subjects were only able to perform the task when dealing with an array that had two or three objects. When the set had more than three objects, Pirahãs' performance on the test was poor.[7] Gordon did not observe any traits typical of inbreeding-related retardation in the Pirahã, and he found them to be competent in performing other tasks. This absence of other explanations gave credence to language as a causative factor for the Pirahãs' limited numeracy skills.

Or, consider Guugu Yimithirr, an indigenous language of Australia. In Guugu Yimithirr, words for spatial relations are nothing like spatial terms in, say, Western languages. When describing large distances, Westerners use terms based on geographic coordinates (e.g., *north, south, east, west*). However, when talking about small spaces, they use coordinates based on the human body, such as *There on your right,* or *Make a step to your right.* Since such person-centric or egocentric words (e.g., *left, right, in front, behind*) are found in a great number of languages, one might expect them to be universal. However, speakers of Guugu Yimithirr *only* describe space in terms of geographic coordinates.[8] Thus, even when describing a small space, they say, *There was someone standing a bit Northwards of me,* or *Make a step a bit Westwards.*

How does this exclusive use of geographic spatial terms impact the spatial cognition of Guugu Yimithirr speakers? Scientists found that speakers of this language had a perfect sense of their position in geographic space. Whether they were indoors or outside, whether they could see the stars or the sun or neither, speakers of Guugu Yimithirr knew exactly where east, west, north, and south were.[9]

In recent years, linguists have also reexamined the effect of language on the cognition of speakers of European languages such as German and Spanish. Can it be that, because they use different words and grammars, speakers of these languages view the world in slightly different ways? In German, for instance, the word for "bridge" is feminine (*die Brücke*), whereas in Spanish it is masculine (*el puente*). As a result, whereas in German a bridge is a *sie* ("she"), in Spanish it is an *él* ("he"). Conversely, the Spanish word for "apple," *la manzana*, is feminine, whereas the German one, *der Apfel*, is masculine. In view of these facts, scientists wondered whether German and Spanish speakers perceived bridges and apples differently. They found that speakers of German did think of bridges as having feminine characteristics such as elegance and slenderness, while Spanish speakers saw them as having masculine traits such as strength. For apples, the effect was reversed.[10]

In spite of such studies, however, few modern scientists espouse the strong formulation of the linguistic relativity hypothesis. Indeed, the notion that language rigidly determines what we can think has been effectively demolished. According to modern linguists, people are able to understand more than they can say because thought is couched not in words but in a mental language, sometimes referred to as *mentalese*. (To understand the notion of mentalese more clearly, try to observe your own thinking. Note that when you engage in thought, you do not necessarily use actual words.) To prove that language does not constrain cognition, scholars also invoke studies demonstrating that children can understand ideas and phenomena that they are unable to convey verbally. For instance, babies and toddlers who are able to follow fairly sophisticated directions are unable to formulate those directions in their own words.

And yet, the evidence from studies of the impact of words on cognition remains compelling. Thus, while modern linguists do not view language as a straitjacket that imposes severe limitations on our thinking, many scientists do believe that having a label for an entity readily available does help us notice and remember that entity.

Words in Context

Imagine a student studying for the verbal section of the SAT. The student is working on a pair of synonyms: *clandestine* and *furtive*. The SAT preparation guide says that the words' respective meanings are "secret, illegal" and "done secretly." The student does not find the definitions helpful enough. She feels that they only scratch the surface of each word's meaning and do not reveal them fully. Why did the student experience these definitions as insufficient?

It is time to make an important point about word meaning: no definition can do an adequate job of describing what a word means.[11] How can this be? First of all, the difficulty in defining word meaning can be accounted for in terms of gestalt theory. You will recall that, according to this theory, the lexical concept is a gestalt; it is whole and indivisible and more than the sum of its parts. When you provide a definition, you deconstruct word meaning or pull it apart. In doing this, you compromise the integrity of meaning and spill some essential semantic information.

Second, a definition does not provide a prototype. You may recall that our mental concepts are hitched to prototypes—examples that represent each concept most typically. The problem with definitions is that they speak in terms of general ideas instead of typical examples.

Third, word meaning is hard to convey via definitions because definitions fail to capture *connotative meaning*, that is, the emotional and cultural associations that words evoke in the speakers' minds.

Is there a way of conveying the full richness of word meaning? Pointing or giving examples—or, as linguists put it, providing an *ostensive definition*—can be helpful. In fact, some words, such as color terms (e.g., *sepia, mauve*) or sensations (e.g., *bitter, tart*) can *only* be explained effectively using ostensive definitions. But ostensive definitions are not always available.

Another helpful strategy is examining the word in *context*, or the broad verbal environment in which a word is used. Let us go back to our two SAT words and consider the following examples:

> Clandestine: *The illegal group met several times in secret locations. Eventually, the CIA blew the cover off these <u>clandestine</u> gatherings.*

> Furtive: *The lovers conducted their affair in secrecy. But whenever they met in public, they could not help stealthily touching hands or exchanging <u>furtive</u> glances.*

Here, contextual clues suggest that whereas *clandestine* refers to organized illicit activity, *furtive* describes physical action.

Second, the nuances of meaning are revealed in *collocations*, or word combinations in which a given word occurs. To appreciate this point, consider Table 4.1. As this table shows, even though *clandestine* and *furtive* are synonyms, they enter different collocations. Each word's unique meaning

TABLE 4.1 Collocations for the Words *Clandestine* and *Furtive*

Word	Common collocations
clandestine	clandestine gathering, clandestine operation, clandestine arm of an organization
furtive	furtive glance, furtive look, furtive behavior

determines how it is paired up with other words. As linguists like to joke, "You shall know a word by the company it keeps."

Implications for Instruction

1. An effective vocabulary lesson focuses on the following: (1) an ostensive or verbal definition, (2) the context in which the word occurs, and (3) the word's collocational properties. Imagine that you need to teach the following target-language items: *to hang out*, *laidback*, and *vicarious*. Create mini-lessons that focus on these words. How will you define their meanings? How will you describe the typical situations or contexts in which they occur? What will you say about these words' collocational properties?

2. Commonly held prototypes can be at odds with scientific findings. For instance, while whales look more like fish than mammals, they share key mammalian characteristics and are, therefore, mammals. Because of the lack of a neat overlap between scientific findings and popular prototypes, scientific concepts may be difficult to teach. How would you go about explaining to students that whales are mammals, and that the sun is a star?

3. Given the metaphorical underpinnings of cognition, it is crucially important to use concrete imagery when teaching complex concepts. Body metaphors make for particularly effective instructional tools. Consider an example. A teacher whose young students were leaving out periods in their writing used a body metaphor to teach this punctuation mark. The teacher told her students that a period "is like a little person crouching on the floor and resting. When words in a sentence get tired of doing their job and need to rest, the period rolls into a little ball and takes a short break." She also explained that, "Once the words are rested, they can stand tall," which is why we use uppercase letters to begin a new sentence. She told her students that an exclamation mark was like a person "jumping up and down with excitement." The class then staged a role-play impersonating the different punctuation marks.

   Can you think of a body metaphor that would help render the concept of a question mark accessible to students? What metaphors could demonstrate the need for lead-in and closure statements in a text? What body metaphors would you use to explain the three states of matter and the interrelation between high temperature and the rapid movement of molecules?

4. Students enjoy activities that illustrate semantic relations between words. For instance, they like to create stories based on synonyms or antonyms.

   Read the poem below. What is the relationship between the underlined words? What conceptual metaphor does the poem illustrate?

   > Mr. Left
   >
   > Mr. Left is a total disgrace,
   > A sore in the eye of the human race.
   > He lives his <u>gauche</u> and <u>sinister</u> life
   > With his <u>left-handed children</u> and <u>left-handed wife.</u>
   > Mr. Left is a kiss-up, a phony, a crook,
   > His <u>left-handed compliments</u> make you puke.
   > The list of his faults is not complete:
   > Mr. Left <u>has two left feet</u>.
   > Arson and treason, murder and theft
   > Are not beneath Mr. Left.

   Develop an instructional activity with a focus on the conceptual metaphor LIFE IS A JOURNEY.

5. Source domains of conceptual metaphors are culture-specific. American English, for instance, has a number of sports-based metaphors (e.g., *drop the ball, hit a home run, step up to the plate*). Develop a mini-lesson with a focus on sports-based American English metaphors.

WORDS TO REMEMBER

semantics: the science of meaning.

referent: the thing or idea represented by a word.

lexical concept: word meaning.

semantic triangle: a model that represents the relationship between a word, its meaning, and its referent.

gestalt: a whole and indivisible mental concept that is more than the sum of its parts.

prototype: the typical, central example in a category.

prototype effect: speakers' perception that some examples in a category are more typical than others.

fuzziness: in semantics, the hazy nature of the periphery of word meaning.

metaphor: using the name for one thing to refer to another thing because of a resemblance between the two.

conceptual metaphor: a common, set expression that compares something abstract to something concrete.

linguistic relativity hypothesis: the hypothesis that language determines thought.

Sapir–Whorf hypothesis: see **linguistic relativity hypothesis**.

mentalese: the language of thought.

connotative meaning: emotional and cultural associations evoked by words.

ostensive definition: clarifying word meaning by pointing out an example.

context: the broad verbal environment in which a word is used.

collocations: word combinations in which a word occurs.

Notes

1. Rosch, E. (1975). Cognitive representations of semantic categories. *Journal of Experimental Psychology: General, 104*(3), 192–233.
2. Armstrong, S. L., Gleitman, L. R., & Gleitman, H. (1983). What some concepts might not be. *Cognition, 13,* 263–308.
3. Lakoff, G., & Johnson, M. (1980). *Metaphors we live by.* Chicago: University of Chicago Press.
4. Reid, T. R. (2000). *Confucius lives next door: What living in the East teaches us about living in the West.* New York: Vintage Random House, pp. 75–79.
5. Sapir, E. (1929). The status of linguistics as a science. *Language, 5*(4), 207–214.
6. Berlin, B., & Kay, P. (1969). *Basic color terms: Their universality and evolution.* Berkeley and Los Angeles: University of California Press.
7. Gordon, P. (2004). Numerical cognition without words: Evidence from Amazonia. *Science, 306,* 496–499.
8. Haviland, I. B. (1979). Guugu Yimidhirr. In R. M. V. Dixon & B. Blake (Eds.), *Handbook of Australian languages* (pp. 27–182). Canberra: Australian National University Press.
9. Levinson, S. (1992). *Language and cognition: The cognitive consequences of spatial description in Guugu Yimithirr* (Working Paper #13). Nijmegen, The Netherlands: Cognitive Anthropology Research Group at the Max Planck Institute of Psycholinguistics.

10. Konishi, T. (1993). The semantics of grammatical gender: A cross-cultural study. *Journal of Psycholinguistic Research, 22,* 519–534.

11. See, e.g., Fodor, J. A, Garret, M. F., Walker, E. C. T., & Parkes, C. H. (1980). Against definitions. *Cognition, 8*(3), 263–367.

5

Pragmatics

Imagine the following situation: a college student enters her dorm room and sees that the message button of her answering machine is flickering. Upon pressing the button, the student hears the following: *"Hello, Alison . . .* [sigh] *How are you?* [sigh] *This is your grandmother calling . . .* [pause] *All right . . .* [sigh, click, silence, dial tone]." This message, left by a native speaker, does not contain any obvious errors. And yet, you have undoubtedly noticed that there is something wrong with it. For one thing, the message lacks a closing statement. It also has too many pauses and is delivered at a pace that the recipient might find insufficiently brisk.

Like Alison's grandmother, we all experience challenges when using language in certain situations. We may struggle with language choices when using an unfamiliar mode of communication—for example, when we first learn to send messages with a new technological tool. Or, we may have difficulty finding the right words to convey a highly sensitive message, such as condolences. These situations, however, are rare. In more common scenarios, we see a different pattern of language use. *"How are you? Hanging in*

there..." "*Hi! It's me. Missed you again. I guess we've been playing phone tag...*"
Chunks of language like these roll off native speakers' tongues.

The study of how speakers use language is the purview of *pragmatics*. What kinds of utterances are used to perform various speech functions? What impact does culture have on the language choices made by speakers? How do speakers interpret these utterances, depending on the context? These are some of the questions examined by pragmatic research.

Pragmatics developed in the 1970s as a reaction to the Chomskian model of language proficiency. At that time, there came the realization that competence, or the tacit mastery of the structural rules of language, does not fully describe language proficiency. Proponents of the new approach argued that the Chomskian paradigm overlooked an important aspect of language proficiency, namely, the speaker's ability to use language in inter-action. The focus in linguistics thus shifted from analysis of the structural makeup of language to an analysis of language as a tool for communication.

Speech Acts

The units of analysis in pragmatics are the *speech act*, the *speech event*, and the *speech community*. A speech act is the act of using language. When speakers say, *I really appreciate that, I apologize, Why don't you call him?*, or *I can't take it anymore*, they are performing speech acts. A speech event is a situation that entails verbal interaction. Examples of speech events include an encounter with a friend, a business meeting, a meal at a restaurant, and a visit to a doctor. A speech community is a group of people who share certain norms of verbal behavior.

Listed below are the names of some select speech acts and the functions they perform:

Expressives (*I was totally overwhelmed.*)—convey emotions;
Directives (*Tell him I said "hi"!*)—make orders or requests;
Comissives (*I am not wearing this.*)—promise or threaten;
Declaratives (*Her name is Yun Jin.*)—provide information.

But what about phrases, such as *Lovely day, isn't it?* or *It is so muggy today.* These utterances do not convey any important content. Rather, they state the obvious. Why do people use them? What function do they perform?

We are social animals, and being at one with a group constitutes one of our fundamental needs. To enforce the bond with fellow humans, we perform speech acts—very much in the way other animals use social grooming or stroking. Phrases such as *Thank God it's Friday! Hot enough for you today?* enable people to maintain *solidarity*, that is, a positive relationship with others.

Phrases speakers use to perform speech acts can be described in terms of their style or *register*. Register can be formal or informal. The social distance between interlocutors, their relative power, and the level of imposition determine speakers' choice of register. For instance, a young child is expected to use an informal register when talking to a parent and a formal one when addressing a teacher. Speakers use different registers when discussing a salary raise with a superior and when asking a friend to give them change for a dollar.

Speech-Act Variety Across Languages

Speech-act behavior varies across cultures. Speakers of different languages have different ways of promising, giving advice, offering food, and complaining.

Consider the case of compliments. While speakers of American English pay compliments quite liberally (e.g., *Nice dress! I love your tie! Great job!*), in other cultures this type of behavior may be considered inappropriate.[1] In some speech communities, a compliment may be suspected of being motivated by a desire for gain. Additionally, in some cultures, there is a belief that a compliment may invite bad luck.

Consequently, ways of receiving compliments vary. In American English, a common response to a compliment is an expression of appreciation. A typical exchange might be as follows:

I like your sneakers.
Thanks. They're comfortable.

However, in other languages, such as Arabic,[2] Chinese,[3] and Russian, a possible response to a compliment is *downgrading*. This strategy involves belittling an item that has drawn a compliment. Thus, after being complimented on an outfit, a speaker of Russian might respond, *Nu, eto staryo!* ("Oh, that's an old rag").

A conversational strategy used in Arabic is that of proffering an item to a complimenter. Upon receiving a compliment, a speaker of Arabic may say, *mgaddam* ("I proffer it to you"), *halaalič* ("It's all yours"), and *ma yi λla áleeč* ("You're worth it"). This strategy is a polite convention, which, though it does not imply that the complimenter will actually take the proffered item, suggests that the complimenter is more deserving of owning the item in question. Another strategy for responding to compliments is the invocation of God, as when speakers of Arabic respond to a compliment by using the formulaic phrase *allay-xaliič* ("May God save you!").[4]

Conventions of performing speech acts are rooted in speakers' cultures. Consider linguist Florian Coulmas's study of Japanese conventions for giving thanks and apologizing.[5] After receiving a gift, an appropriate English response would be a token of gratitude such as *Thank you* or *I really appreciate it.* Speakers of Japanese, however, say *sumimasen*, a formulaic utterance that is also used to perform the speech act of apology and literally means "it never ends" (i.e., "I am aware of my never-ending indebtedness to you"). In the same vein, upon leaving a dinner party a Japanese person might say, *O-jamaitashishimashita* ("I have intruded on you"). Coulmas notes that ritualistic apologies are pervasive in the Japanese language and that they occur "even when there was no serious or real offence as a precaution against inadvertent or unanticipated negative interpretation of one's performance."[6] The use of apologies to express gratitude is deeply rooted in the Japanese culture, which places great emphasis on being considerate to others and repaying debt. By apologizing while expressing gratitude, the speaker begs forgiveness for any trouble she may have inadvertently caused.

Let us consider a few more conversational formulae that capture various cultural experiences. In Turkey and Greece, two seafaring cultures, there is an ingrained concern for the welfare of travelers. When a speaker of Turkish or Greek learns that someone close to the speaker is about to embark on a trip, she typically exclaims, *Allah kavuştursun* ("May God reunite") (in Turkish) or *kali andamosi* ("Good meeting") (in Greek). Other common phrases reference the concept of the evil eye, which is reportedly very powerful in this region. Thus, mention of a good event almost never passes without the use of some accompanying formula, for example:

Allah nazardan saklasin (Turkish: "May God protect from the evil eye")
Na mi vaskathis (Greek: "May you not be touched by the evil eye")[7]

People's behavior at mealtimes is laden with cultural meaning, and it is only natural that speech acts performed at mealtimes have attracted the attention of scientists. One study, by Polish-Australian linguist Anna Wierzbicka, compared utterances used for offering food in English and Eastern European languages, such as Polish and Russian. Wierzbicka noted that English speakers, when offering food to a houseguest, typically use questions such as *Would you like some salad?* or *Would you like a beer?* She explains that, to speakers of Eastern European languages, couching an offer of food in a question sounds distant and cold. Instead, the social conventions of Polish culture require the host "to prevail upon the guest, to behave as if he or she was forcing the guest to eat and drink, regardless of the guest's desires and certainly regardless of the guest's expressed desires which would be simply dismissed."[8] According to this cultural scenario, the host implores the guest to eat, the guest refuses, and the host keeps insisting. A typical dialogue might run as follows:

> *Proszę bardzo!* ("Please have a little more!")
> *Ale juz ne mogę!* ("But I can't!")
> *Ale koniecznie!* ("But you must!")

Note that even the grammar of a speech act has cultural significance. The English use of questions when offering food is a case in point. By using the interrogative utterance (e.g., *Would you like some tea?*), the speaker of English conveys a message of not intruding on the space of the addressee and giving him or her the option of refusing.

There are, of course, many other morphosyntactic means of achieving pragmatic effects. Spanish, for instance, makes ample use of the diminutive suffix *-ita*. When added to the end of a noun or pronoun (e.g., *tacita* ["little cup"]), the diminutive suffix conveys a message of intimacy and friendliness. One study reports that, when asking a neighbor to borrow a cup of sugar or the like, a speaker of Spanish would use the form *tacita* ("little cup"), not *taza* ("cup"). Such a friendly, casual request would thus run as follows: *Me puede prestar una tacita de azúcar?* ("Could I borrow a cup of sugar?"). As linguist Martha Mendoza explains,

> One does not ask someone: *Hazme un favor* but *Hazme un favorcito* ("Do me a favor"), which is not to say that it will be a small one; indeed, one might be asking a lot. Or one can say, *Quisiera hablarle de un asuntillo* ("I would like to talk to you about something") so as not to appear too imposing. And the beggar on the street would request: *Una limosnita, por favor* ("Spare some change, please"), making use of diminutive forms, in order to come across as non-threatening and at the same time elicit the hearer's compassion.[9]

Diminutive suffixes exist in English as well; consider such words as *kitchenette* and *cigarette*. The English suffix *-ette*, however, is not nearly as pervasive as the Spanish *-ita*, nor do English words with diminutive suffixes have any special emotional connotations. In contrast, many other languages, including those as different from each other as Arabic, Cantonese, Dutch, Polish, Greek, and Russian, make ample use of diminutive suffixes to convey a message of intimacy.

It is important to bear in mind that not only speech etiquette is culture specific. Speakers of different languages also have different ways of professing love, philosophizing, praying, and so on. Another study by Wierzbicka looked at the different ways speakers of Russian and English converse about friendship, freedom, homeland, and human personality. Wierzbicka analyzed words commonly used by speakers of Russian for criticism and approbation (e.g., *podlec* ["scoundrel"], *negodjaj* ["villain"], *merzavec* ["dishonorable person"], *blagorodny* ["noble person"], and *velikodushnaja* ["magnanimous"]) and compared them to English words used for characterization. Wierzbicka came to the conclusion that, whereas English characterization words tend to be more understated and pragmatic, Russian ones are more likely to convey moral judgment. In the researcher's own words, "Russians are as extreme and emotional in expressing moral enthusiasm as they are in expressing moral condemnations."[10]

Conversational Routines

While speech act behavior varies across cultures, there are pragmatic properties shared by all languages. One such pragmatic universal is the use of *conversational formulae* or *conversational routines*, that is, set, formulaic expressions. Languages are replete with formulae, which, though lacking in flexibility, enable us to interact efficiently and with minimal effort.

Conversational formulae are predictable on different levels. First of all, they are often fixed phonologically. Phrases such as the sardonic *Yeah, right...* or the contemplative *It is what it is...* or the incredulous *Wow! That's crazy!* are each delivered with a highly distinctive intonation pattern.

Furthermore, speech formulae tend to be fixed on the grammatical level. English polite requests, for instance, are often couched in the form of a question (e.g., *Can you pass the salt?* or *Would you mind passing the salt?*). Alternative syntactic patterns are highly unlikely. If at a dinner table someone said to you, *Pass the salt, please!* you would most probably feel that the person was being rude.

The wording of speech formulae is immutable. Take the phrases *Yeah, I know...*, *I see*, and *I get it*, which are all used for the purpose of *backchanneling*, or responding to an utterance. It is very unlikely for a speaker to change these phrases and say, for instance, *I comprehend*.

Finally, speech events consist of strings of speech acts that tend to follow a script. Consider the scripted cues in the speech act of apologizing:

I am so sorry!
Don't worry about it.

Or an exchange between a salesperson and a patron:

Will that be cash or charge?
Cash, please.
That will be $25.99. $4.01 is your change.

The Meaning of Speech Acts

Imagine you are at a party. You have been approached by a friend who asks, *When are you leaving?* Analyzed at face value, this question is an information request. However, you know that your friend does not own a car and interpret her question as a request for a ride; your response is, *I'm leaving at 10:00. Do you need a ride?* Your friend looks relieved. You understood her and complied with her indirectly stated request.

As you can see, a speech act has two meanings: the surface meaning and the real, intended meaning. The intended meaning arises in context. It is construed by interlocutors based on contextual clues, the shared knowledge of the world and shared cultural expectations. Understanding an utterance involves understanding its intended meaning. An utterance's surface meaning is known as its *locutionary content*; its real, intended meaning is called *illocutionary force*.

Speakers do not need to construe the illocutionary force of a speech act in each and every case. The illocutionary force of some utterances is fixed by cultural conventions. Conversational formulae, also known as conversational routines, are cases in point. Table 5.1 lists some examples of conversational routines and their conventional interpretations.

TABLE 5.1 Locutionary Content and Illocutionary Force of Some Conversational Formulae

Conversational routine	Context	Locutionary content	Illocutionary force
How are you?	Meeting	Information question	Greeting
What's up?	Meeting	Information question	Greeting
Is Sybil there?	Telephone conversation	Information question	Request

Meta-Pragmatic Knowledge

The term *meta-pragmatic knowledge* refers to the speaker's awareness of her own patterns of language use. Native speakers' meta-pragmatic knowledge is imperfect. They use conversational routines or formulae without registering what they say or when and how they say it. This is not to deny that certain phrases—especially those associated with verbal etiquette—are used consciously. Members of speech communities are very aware of the wording of apologies, thanks, polite requests, and other similar phrases. Indeed, children are often explicitly instructed in the use of appropriate formulae such as *Thank you, I'm sorry,* and *May I have it?* That said, there are many more phrases that are used and learned unconsciously.

Consider some examples of *conversational gambits,* that is, phrases used to initiate, sustain, and finish conversational exchanges. When users of American English wish to wrap up a conversation, they use the word *anyway* with a little pause, and a distinctly elongated first vowel: *A-a-anyway.* . . . In this context, *anyway* serves the purpose of letting the interlocutor know that the conversation is about to end; it gives the speaker an effective strategy for winding down the exchange without being rude. Or, consider another conversational gambit, the word *actually* used to express polite disagreement, as when one person says, *Sidney is the capital of Australia,* and another replies, *Actually, it's Canberra.* It is safe to say that speakers are not specifically instructed to use the conversational gambit *anyway* and *actually.* People pick up and use these strategies unconsciously, just like hundreds of other formulae that enable smooth conversation.

Speakers' lack of awareness about their own patterns of language use may seem odd, but there is an explanation for it. What's important to remember is that conversational routines are part of our culture. Even though every manifestation of our behavior is culturally mediated, we are hardly aware of our culture's influence; indeed, we think it is only natural to act the way we do. Given that the rules of language use are a subset of our cultural norms, it shouldn't be surprising that we use them automatically. It is only when we have a cross-cultural encounter, as when we go overseas or interact with a language learner, that differences in language use begin to catch our attention.

Pragmatic Competence

The mastery of conventions of language use is termed *pragmatic competence* or *pragmatic proficiency.* Generally, young second-language learners have little difficulty in developing pragmatic competence. They quickly pick up conversational routines and use them with facility. In her study of second-language development, Lily Wong Fillmore reports that children immersed in a second language are particularly quick in acquiring speech acts needed for play.[11] Teachers who work with young ESL students marvel at how swiftly and accurately children learn to use phrases that satisfy their immediate needs. When young language learners acquire formulae such as *I'm telling on you! Do you want to be my friend? He's bothering me!* and *No fair!*, they use them in appropriate situations and with near-native intonation.

Children may, however, experience some difficulty with conversational strategies used for interacting with adults. An aspect of second-language pragmatics that young language learners find particularly challenging is the use of appropriate forms of address.[12] For instance, distinguishing between polite and informal pronouns, the so-called T and V forms (from the French *tu* and *vous*), may confound youngsters. They may have particular difficulty mastering such forms of address if their home language lacks either the T or the V form, or else uses them differently. In the school setting, young language learners may use the norms of their home language, when addressing the teacher. For instance, a Korean- or Spanish-speaking child might say, *Teacher! I need help.* In so doing, the young language learner resorts to the conversational strategy in use in his or her home language, where students address the teacher using the word *profesora* (in Spanish) or *seon-saeng-nim* (in Korean). This use of home-language cultural norms when speaking a second language is known as *negative pragmatic transfer.*

Language learners make pragmatic errors because they fail to notice certain formulae used by native speakers.[13] The chances of missing a foreign-language speech act are particularly great if no similar strategy is found in the language learners' mother tongue. Thus, language learners may miss certain common expressions such as *Excuse the mess, Thank you for having me!*, and *Do you have a minute?* If they underuse formulae of politeness, language learners may strike native speakers as being rude.

Even when language learners are aware of the target culture's communication conventions, they may struggle with using the target forms. The norms for home-language speech-act behavior are so deeply ingrained that language learners may feel uncomfortable adopting a new cultural script. A study found that female Japanese learners of English feel uncomfortable about refusing in English because this strategy is discouraged in Japanese society. As one learner explained:

I'm no good at—um—saying no [...]—because I I haven't never—I I haven't learned saying no [...] this is our Japanese custom—uh—um—any times uh um—my family taught me—uh smile and—modest and uh—is the attitude is to be—not—not say—no—is very uh—good part—to uh women—Japanese women—sometimes [laughs] and—it's easy to control and we can keep our—our harmony—with uh many people.[14]

Once language learners have learned a strategy, they may initially overuse it. While native speakers use a variety of forms for greetings, thanks, and apologies, the language learner will reiterate the only one she has mastered.[15] Using the full range of speech registers may also present a challenge to second-language learners. Because learners have not yet mastered the entire gamut of conversational styles, native speakers may find learners' speech either too formal or too informal.

It is hardly surprising that language learners can be reticent and speak too little, but they can also be excessively verbose. The predilection of certain language learners for speaking a lot is known as *gushing*. It is as if a language learner feels compelled to use the new language and to practice newly learned patterns. Here is one language learner's witty account of her tendency to gush:

Soon I talked up the English storm. [...] *Cat got your tongue? No big deal! So there! Take that! Holy Toledo!* (Our teacher's favorite "curse word.") *Go jump in the lake! Really dumb. Golly.* Slang, clichés, sayings, hot-shot language that our teachers called, ponderously, idiomatic expressions. Riddles, jokes, puns, conundrums. *What is yellow and goes click-click? Why did the chicken cross the road? See you later, alligator.* How wonderful to call someone an alligator and not be scolded for being disrespectful. In fact, they were supposed to say back, *In a while, crocodile.*[16]

Because speech acts are semantically complex, both young and adult second language learners may experience difficulty in understanding them. This difficulty arises because language learners lack the cultural knowledge needed for interpreting some utterances and construing their intended meaning. Since language learners are not yet fully familiar with the conventions of target-language use, they tend to process the locutionary content, but not the illocutionary force, of common formulae. For instance, a language learner may misinterpret the phrase *How are you?* as an information request or the question *Do you have the time?* as an inquiry of whether one has some time to spare.

A striking example of processing speech-act meaning on the locutionary level and missing its illocutionary force is reported in a study that focuses on Japanese language learners:

> The "please help yourself" that Americans use so often had a rather unpleasant ring in my ears before I became used to English conversation. The meaning, of course, is simply "please take what you want without hesitation," but literally translated it has somehow a flavor of of "nobody will help you," and I could not see how it came to be an expression of good will.[17]

Sometimes, language learners who do not fully grasp the illocutionary force of target speech acts make biased assumptions about the target-language culture. For instance, language learners have told their ESL teacher that they find speakers of English insincere and insensitive because they ask, *Are you OK?* when they see someone in trouble. "Why ask, *Are you OK?*", lamented one language learner, "in a situation when it is perfectly clear that I am not?"[18] This ESL student had processed the locutionary content of the speech act, but not its illocutionary force, and did not realize that the utterance she perceived as being disingenuous was in fact an expression of concern, not a request for information.

Implications for Instruction

1. Teaching pragmatic competence is particularly effective when language teachers become adept at observing actual communication and recording speech patterns used by native speakers. Observe utterances used for (a) leaving a phone message, (b) inviting a friend to a family dinner, (c) offering someone a ride, and (d) asking for directions while driving. Develop activities with a focus on these language items.

2. Emailing and text messaging are examples of relatively new speech genres. Identify some language patterns that are associated with these new modes of communication.

3. English conversational formulae that describe feelings are often couched in the passive voice (e.g., *I was really impressed, I was totally overwhelmed, I'm so excited!*). Think of similar phrases and the situations in which they might be used. Create role-playing lessons that focus on the use of the conversational formulae above.

4. Language-teaching curricula are particularly effective when they focus on learners' communicative needs. The language learner may need to be able to make a complaint to a landlord, describe her impressions of a movie, or criticize a political situation in her

country. Which formulae are commonly used to perform these particular speech acts? *Gambits*

5. Given that language learners often have difficulty using the appropriate register, create a lesson that focuses on making requests or invitations using informal and formal conversational styles.

WORDS TO REMEMBER

pragmatics: study of language in use.

meta-pragmatic knowledge: the speaker's awareness of her own patterns of language use.

pragmatic competence: mastery of the cultural conventions of language use.

negative pragmatic transfer: applying L1 norms of language use when speaking L2.

speech act: an act of using language to perform a communicative function.

speech event: a situation in which speakers use one or several speech acts.

speech community: a group of people with shared norms for verbal interaction.

register: a conversational style (e.g., informal, formal) used by a speaker.

solidarity function: using language to establish a positive relationship with others.

downgrading: responding to a compliment by belittling an item that has drawn a compliment.

backchanneling: responding to an utterance.

conversational gambits: phrases used to initiate, sustain, and finish conversational exchanges.

conversational routine/formula: a culturally conventionalized set expression used to perform a communicative function.

locutionary content: the surface meaning of a speech act.

illocutionary force: a speech act's intended meaning that arises in context.

gushing: the overuse of an L2 form or excessive verbosity exhibited by language learners.

Notes

1. Wolfson, N. (1989). *Perspectives: Sociolinguistics and TESOL.* New York: Newbury House.
2. Farghal, M., & Haggan, M. (2006). Compliment behavior in bilingual Kuwaiti college students. *International Journal of Bilingual Education and Bilingualism, 9*(1), 114.
3. Yu, M. (2005). Sociolinguistic competence in the complimenting act of native Chinese and American English speakers: A mirror of cultural value. *Language and Speech, 48*(1), 91–119.
4. Farghal, M., & Haggan, M. (2006). Compliment behavior in bilingual Kuwaiti college students. *International Journal of Bilingual Education and Bilingualism, 9*(1), 114.
5. Coulmas, F. (1981). "Poison to your soul": Thanks and apologies contrastively viewed. In F. Coulmas (Ed.), *Conversational routine: Explorations in standardized communication situations and prepatterned speech* (pp. 69–91). The Hague, The Netherlands: Mouton.
6. Ibid, p. 84.
7. Tannen, D., & Oztek, P. C. (1981). Health to our mouths: Formulaic expressions in Turkish and Greek. In F. Coulmas (Ed.), *Conversational routines: Explorations in standardized communication situations and prepatterned speech* (pp. 37–54). The Hague, The Netherlands: Mouton.
8. Wierzbicka, A. (1991). *Cross-cultural pragmatics: The semantics of human interaction* (Vol. 53). Berlin: Mouton de Gruyer, p. 28.
9. Mendoza, M. (2005). Polite diminutives in Spanish: A matter of size? In R. Lakoff & I. Sachiko (Eds.), *Broadening the horizon of linguistic politeness* (pp. 163–173). Amsterdam: John Benjamins.
10. Wierzbicka, A. (1992). *Semantics, culture and cognition: Universal human concepts in culture-specific configuration.* New York: Oxford University Press, p. 439.
11. Fillmore, L. (1976). *The second time around: Cognitive and social strategies in second language acquisition.* Unpublished doctoral dissertation, Stanford University, Stanford, CA.
12. Brown, R., & Gillman, A. (1960). The pronouns of power and solidarity. In T. A. Sebeok (Ed.), *Style in language* (pp. 253–276). Cambridge, MA: MIT Press.
13. Bardovi-Harlig, K. (2009). Conventional expressions as a pragmalinguistic resource: Recognition and production of conventional expressions in L2 pragmatics. *Language Learning 59*(4), 755–795.
14. Robinson, M. (1992). Introspective methodology in interlanguage pragmatic research. In G. Kasper (Ed.), *Pragmatics of Japanese as native and target language.* Technical Report No. 3, Second Language Teaching and Curriculum Center, University of Hawaii at Manoa, pp. 27–82. Cited in Kasper. G. (1992). Pragmatic transfer. *Second Language Research, 8*(3), 214.
15. Bardovi-Harlig, K. (2009). Conventional expressions as a pragmalinguistic resource: Recognition and production of conventional expressions in L2 pragmatics. *Language Learning 59*(4), 755–795.
16. Alvalrez, J. (1998). *Something to declare: Essays.* New York: Penguin Putnam, pp. 24–25.

17. Doi, T. (1973). *The anatomy of dependence.* Cited in Coulmas, F. (1981). Introduction: Conversational routine. In F. Coulmas (Ed.), *Conversational routine: Explorations in standardized communication situations and prepatterned speech* (pp. 11–19). The Hague, The Netherlands: Mouton.
18. Gordon, T. (1991). Personal communication with a student.

6

Neurolinguistics

This chapter discusses findings in *neurolinguistics*, the field of research that investigates how the brain is organized for language. Most neurolinguistics studies have focused on the structure of the *cortex*, a grayish outer sheet of brain cells that controls language memory, voluntary action, and consciousness. What methods do scientists use to study the cortex?

In the early years of neurolinguistics, the brain could not be observed in "real time." The only research method available to scientists in those days was the post-mortem examination of the people who suffered from *aphasia*, a congenital or acquired speech disorder. When an aphasia patient died, the brain was dissected and the location of a *lesion* (damaged brain tissue) was indentified. By using this procedure in several similar cases, scientists were able to establish which brain region controlled the impaired language function.

More recently scientists have been using *dichotic tests.* These tests rely on the fact that our brains' control of our bodies is contralateral, with the left hemisphere predominantly sending signals to the right side of the body, and vice versa. Under normal conditions, this contralateral manage-

The Educator's Guide to Linguistics, pages 79–91
Copyright © 2012 by Information Age Publishing
All rights of reproduction in any form reserved.

ment of speech stimuli is of no consequence. However, when we experience stimulus overload, the dominance of one hemisphere becomes apparent. For instance, when researchers send auditory verbal stimuli into both ears at exactly the same time, study participants consistently hear better with their right ear. Thus, if the subject *simultaneously* hears the words *one, three,* and *five* in her right ear, and *two, seven,* and *nine* in her left, she is likely to miss *two, seven,* or *nine.* This suggests that the left hemisphere is dominant for processing auditory signals. Similarly, scientists perform *dichoptic tests,* simultaneously flashing several written words in the subject's left and right visual fields. In the dichoptic tests, the subject is more likely to process the word on her right. Dichotic and dichoptic tests have enabled scientists to determine which hemisphere is dominant in language processing.

In recent years, scientists have been able to take advantage of innovative brain-imaging techniques such as *magnetic resonance imaging* (MRI) and *positron emission technology* (PET) scans. By registering the flow of blood to different areas of the brain, researchers are able to tell which one has been activated. Both MRIs and PET scans produce successions of images that show brain activity over time.

Lateralization and Localization

A groundbreaking early neurolinguistic discovery was made in 1861 by a French neurologist Paul Broca. Broca studied a patient who came to be known as "Tan Tan" in the scholarly literature. Broca's patient, a stroke victim paralyzed on his right side, got his nickname because he could only utter one word: "tan." Tan Tan pronounced that single word with varying intonation and appeared to be irritated by his inability to say more.

When Tan Tan died, Broca performed an autopsy on his brain. He discovered that his patient had a hollow space filled with liquid in the cortex, near the left temple. Broca went on to perform postmortem examinations on eight more patients with similar language impairments and found that they all had lesions in the cortical area, always near the left temple. This region of the brain has come to be called *Broca's area* (see Figure 6.2); the language deficit caused by a lesion located in this area is known as *Broca's aphasia.*

Consider the speech sample produced by a Broca's aphasia patient who had been asked to describe the Cookie Theft picture used in language testing (Figure 6.1):

Copyright © 1983 by Lee & Febiger

Figure 6.1   Cookie Theft picture. (Published with permission from ProEd.)

kid...kk...can...candy...cookie...candy...well I don't know but it's
writ...easy does it...slam...early...fall...men...many no...girl. dishes...soap...soap...water...water...falling pah that's all...dish...that's
all.   cookies...can...candy...cookies   cookies...he...down...That's
all. Girl...slipping water...and it hurts...much to do...Her...clean
up...Dishes...up there...I think that's doing it [The examiner asks: What
is she doing with the dishes?] discharge no...I forgot...dirtying clothes
[?] dish [?] water...[The examiner probes: What about it?] slippery water...[?] scolded...slipped.[1]

The patient's speech is full of pauses and is delivered in disjointed bits.
Because this condition is accompanied by the impairment of articulation,
the sufferer speaks with great effort; his speech is slow and deliberate.

Broca'a aphasia is accompanied by the breakdown of grammar. The
afflicted person loses the use of bound morphemes, such as plurality markers and also function words, such as auxiliaries, conjunctions, or pronouns.
The aphasiac will understand the noun *oar*, but be unable to recognize the
conjunction *or*; will use and recognize the noun *eye*, but be unable to use
the pronoun *I*. Broca's aphasics also have difficulty with word retrieval. If
somebody asked you to think of words that you associate with a meal, you
would have no trouble producing a list of words such as *food, drink, eat, plate,*

knife, fork, and so on. Broca's aphasics, however, have difficulty producing thematically framed word lists of this sort.

Because it affects both fluency and control of grammar, Broca's aphasia is also known as *nonfluency disorder* and *agrammatism.* This condition primarily affects speech production, with comprehension being spared. Aphasiacs are aware of their condition and respond to treatment.

Another important early nerolinguistic discovery was made in 1874 by German neurologist Carl Wernicke. Wernicke performed a postmortem examination on aphasics who had lesions in the cortical area of the left brain, in the region close to the left ear (Figure 6.2). This region, now called *Wernicke's area,* plays an important part in speech comprehension. The speech processing impairment that results from congenital or acquired damage to Wernicke's area is called *Wernicke's aphasia.*

Below is an excerpt from the speech of A.M., a 75-year-old sufferer from Wernicke's aphasia. The examiner's interpretations of this patient's speech are in square brackets:

> Is this some of the work that we work as we did before?...All right...From when wine [why] I'm here. What's wrong with me because I...was myself until the tanz took something about the time between me and my regular time in that time and they took the time in that time here and that's when the the time took around here and saw me around in it it's started with me no time and then I bekan [began] work of nothing else that's the way the doctor find me that way....[2]

The speech sample above is quite different from that of a Broca's aphasiac. The sentences are well formed and flow effortlessly. However, the

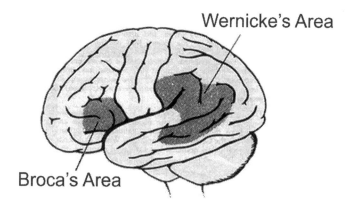

Figure 6.2   The localization of Broca's and Wernicke's areas in the left hemisphere.

utterance includes invented or mispronounced words (e.g., *tanz, bekan*); most importantly, it is void of meaningful content.

In marked contrast to Broca's aphasiacs, Wernicke's aphasics' ability to comprehend language is severely impaired. These aphasics are unable to understand the speech of others, and their own speech makes no sense. The effortlessly flowing speech of Wernicke aphasics often includes made-up, nonexistent words as well as *circumlocution*, elaborate, roundabout ways of saying things. Wernicke's aphasia is a severe impairment; those afflicted do not respond to treatment.

Given the localization of Broca's and Wernicke's areas in the left hemisphere, scientists speak of the *lateralization* of language function; that is, the predominant involvement of the left hemisphere in controlling language. Left-hemisphere language lateralization is found not only in hearing individuals, but also in deaf persons who use sign language. While not all people have language in their left hemisphere, most do. Language is located in the left brain in 95% of right-handed and 80% of left-handed individuals.

But what about the right hemisphere? What role, if any, does it play in language use? Before we answer this question, a few words are in order about the overall differentiation of functions between the two hemispheres. The left and the right parts of the brain tend to play different roles in cognition. While the left hemisphere is responsible for analytical thinking, logical reasoning, and distinguishing between entities, the right hemisphere is in charge of synthesis. The right brain contributes to our ability to recognize things and note similarities between them.

Because the right hemisphere plays a role in recognition, people with severe damage to the right brain lose the ability to identify objects. In his book *The Man Who Mistook his Wife for a Hat*, neurologist Oliver Sacks describes his patient Dr. P., who had severe right-hemisphere damage:

> 'What is this?' I asked, holding up a glove. 'May I examine it?' he asked, and, taking it from me, he proceeded to examine it as he had examined the geometrical shapes. 'A continuous surface,' he announced at last,'infolded on itself. It appears to have'—he hesitated—'five outpouchings, if this is the word.' 'Yes,' I said cautiously. 'You have given me a description. Now tell me what it is.' 'A container of some sort?' 'Yes,' I said, 'and what would it contain?' 'It would contain its contents!' said Dr P., with a laugh. 'There are many possibilities. It could be a change purse, for example, for coins of five sizes. It could...' I interrupted the barmy flow. 'Does it not look familiar? Do you think it might contain, might fit, a part of your body?' No light of recognition dawned on his face.[3]

As is clear from the passage above, Dr. P retained the use of language, but was unable to recognize a common object, in this instance, a glove.

The right hemisphere also plays a dominant role in our ability to express and perceive feelings. The production and the interpretation of facial expressions, for instance, are controlled by the right hemisphere.

Because of its link to affect, the right hemisphere plays an important part in language use. There is evidence, for instance, that it controls our ability to produce intonation. People who suffer from damage to the right hemisphere exhibit so-called *flat affect*. They speak in a monotone and have difficulty conveying emotions, such as anger or enthusiasm.[4] Damage to the right hemisphere may also have an adverse affect on an individual's ability to interpret intonation. [5]

Some studies suggest that the right brain may contribute to our ability to draw complex inferences. For instance, individuals with right-hemisphere damage may have difficulty making complex interpretations[6] and understanding metaphorical language.[7] Thus, a patient who suffered from a right-brain injury may understand the direct meanings of the words *cold* and *warm*, while being unable to understand phrases such as *a warm reception* or *a cold person*.

As this discussion makes clear, there exists a certain amount of autonomy among the brain regions that control different speech functions. For instance, people can lose the ability to control grammar but still be able to comprehend language (Broca's aphasia); or, they may be able to produce speech that is fluent but void of meaningful content (Wernicke's aphasia). Yet another possibility is that an individual whose ability to produce and comprehend language is relatively unimpaired may suffer from a breakdown in the affective component of speech.

The view that different language functions are independent of each other because they are controlled by different brain regions is known as the *localization hypothesis*. To assume this hypothesis in its strongest form would be a gross simplification. There is ample evidence that the organization of language is not strictly confined to specific areas of the brain. And yet, the localization hypothesis is not to be dismissed. It helps explain why people can retain control of some language skills while losing the ability to exercise others.

Brain Circuitry in Bilinguals

Is there any difference in the neural circuitry of pre- and post-pubescent language learners? A study conducted at Cornell University in New York

State has provided some initial data.[8] Using fMRIs, the Cornell researchers were able to observe brain activity during language production in two types of learners. Of the 12 bilingual subjects who participated in the study, half had learned their second language at a young age, half during adolescence. The subjects were asked to describe what they had done the day before: first, using their mother tongue; then, using their second language.

The researchers discovered that their subjects' brains operated differently depending on whether they had learned their second language early or late. Those subjects who had become bilingual at a young age used the same part of Broca's area for both languages. In contrast, late learners used one part of Broca's area for first-language sentences and a different, adjacent part of Broca's area when speaking in their second language. The researchers did not observe any difference in the functioning of Wernicke's area: both late and early language learners used the same part of the brain to understand language.

Another study conducted at Georgetown University has focused on the use of memory in late and early language learners. Michael Ullman, a Georgetown University-based neuroscientist, is investigating the question of whether we use declarative or procedural memory for language learning.

You may recall that *declarative memory* is used to remember new facts and events, while *procedural memory* is in charge of motor skills, such as riding a bike or swimming. The two types of memory work differently. While procedural memory tends to be durable, declarative memory often fails us. We remember, for instance, how to swim or ride a bike even when we haven't practiced these skills in years, but we are unable to recall many facts we learned at school.

After examining various psycholinguistic and neurolinguistic data, Ullman came to an interesting conclusion. According to Ullman, procedural memory is involved in grammar learning in children. However, when learning new words, children rely on declarative memory. Grammar learning in children seems to be like learning to ride a bike, while word learning is like learning the capital of Delaware (it's Dover). When it comes to adult language learners, however, the picture seems to be different. Whether late learners are learning an unfamiliar language's words or grammar, they do so by relying on their declarative memory.[9]

Co-Speech Gestures

This part of the chapter discusses *co-speech gestures*—that is, hand movements that are synchronized with speech and related to its content. Co-speech gestures must be distinguished from other hand movements, such as adjusting one's hair or rubbing one's chin, which can occur independently of speech.

There are four kinds of co-speech gestures. First, there are *iconic*, or representational, gestures. These gestures provide a visual portrayal of entities. For instance, when describing a coiled spring, the speaker is likely to make a spiral motion with her index finger.

Another, related group of co-speech gestures is *deictic gestures*. When these are performed, the speaker points to something with a hand or a finger. Deictic gestures commonly accompany giving directions or identifying objects.

Third, there are *emblematic gestures*. These are gestures that conventionally signify certain meanings. Flashing a peace sign, waving a hand in the air in greeting, or extending a thumb as a sign of approval are examples of emblematic gestures.

The fourth type of gestures are *beats*. These are repetitive hand motions that people perform while speaking. Beats are noniconic and do not point; they are used for emphasis or to underscore speech rhythm.[10]

Why do people use gestures? Consider two examples. First, imagine the speaker giving directions about the placement of furniture: "*Just lean the mirror against the wall over here* [index finger indicating the place where the mirror needs to be placed]." Second, imagine the speaker describe a hairstyle: "*She has bangs,* [downward motion with two hands in front of the forehead] *and a shoulder-long pageboy cut* [shoulder-swiping hand movements]."

In the two situations just described, deictic and iconic gestures help both the speaker and the addressee elucidate and process speech content. As you may recall, words are arbitrary. There is nothing about the forms of the words *over there, bangs, pageboy haircut* that reflects their meaning. In contrast, many co-speech gestures are iconic or picture-like. When such gestures are used, each small hand movement conjures up an image that clarifies the message.[11]

There is ample research evidence that hand gestures help an individual on the receiving end of verbal communication. Listeners are more likely to process and retain information if the speaker gesticulates while talking. In experimental studies, actors told stories with and without gestures. When gestures were used, listeners' recall of the story was better.[12]

But if the only purpose of co-speech gestures were to clarify the meaning of utterances, why would speakers move their hands even when no one else is around? Why do we gesticulate when speaking over the phone? Why do actors or radio announcers move their hands when talking into a microphone? Why do congenitally blind children use gestures when speaking? Even more intriguingly, why do blind children gesticulate when talking to other blind children?[13]

Today, we have ample evidence that all kinds of co-speech gestures (whether they be icons or beats) play a role in speech production. It has been demonstrated that when people are prevented from moving their hands, they speak with greater effort. Conversely, when speakers are able to gesture, they speak more fluently.[14] There is also evidence that hand movement aids word retrieval.[15] If a speaker uses a hand gesture to portray word meaning, she has less difficulty recalling that word.[16] For instance, a respondent will be asked to name a "calculating tool consisting of a wooden frame and beads sliding on a wire" or "a slender, pointed missile, often having tail fins, thrown by hand or shot from a blowgun." When speakers pretend to slide beads across a wire or, when they put their thumb and index finger together, they take less time naming the *abacus* and the *dart*. Moreover, there is evidence that *any* hand motion, even just tapping rhythmically, helps with word recall.[17]

The studies of the impact of gestures on language learning have also provided some important results. We know, for instance, that in children gestural and language development are tightly bound.[18] We also know that more proficient second language learners are more likely to use gestures[19] and that gesturing helps second word retention and recall.[20] When teaching of a new Japanese word is coupled with a demonstration (e.g., the teacher producing a drinking gesture while saying, "*nomu* means drink"), students are more likely to remember the word.

But how do studies in neurolinguistics account for the link between gestures and language? Research answers to these questions have been truly revealing. Recent brain-imaging studies have demonstrated that Broca's area and other brain areas implicated in language production and comprehension also play a role in the comprehension and production of co-speech gestures.[21] Given this evidence, scientists argue that gestures can serve as a powerful language teaching tool that enhances language development.[22]

Mirror Neurons

A glimpse of a new direction in brain-imaging research has been offered by studies launched in Italy in the first decade of this century. The first stages of the research were inauspicious. In the city of Parma, scientists were studying the brain neurons (i.e., brain cells) of macaque monkeys. They were interested in finding out which neurons fired or were activated when the monkeys performed physical actions. The scientists observed that every time the monkey performed an action, such as reaching for a peanut, neurons fired in the premotor area. Then, by sheer accident, scientists noticed that the same neurons fired when the monkey observed a researcher take a peanut. This was a stunning finding. It meant that whether the monkey performed an action or saw somebody else perform the same action, the same mirror neurons were firing. It was later discovered that the same neurons even fired when the monkey *heard* a peanut being taken.

The Italian scientists called these newly discovered neurons *mirror neurons*. The discovery of mirror neurons suggests that the monkeys' brains dissolve the difference between action and the perception of action. The localization of these brain cells is intriguing. The scientists found that mirror neurons in monkeys are localized in an area similar to Broca's area in humans.

So far scientists have been unable to observe single neurons in humans. However, scientists did observe mirror brain activation in the frontal area when subjects performed an action or read a sentence that described that action.[23] For instance, the brain reacted similarly when a person took a peach or read a sentence that said "She took a peach." Because the area of mirror activation is located close to Broca's area, scientists have speculated that mirror neurons have a role in language acquisition.[24]

Implications for Instruction

1. The localization hypothesis, challenges common misconceptions about language teaching. Caretakers and educators tend to assume that the development of one language skill will automatically contribute to the development of another one. For instance, there is a widely held belief that if a child spends a lot of time reading, her writing ability is likely to be boosted. In actuality, the interrelation between our receptive and productive language skills is relatively weak. Not all avid readers are proficient writers, and an articulate person can experience problems with comprehension. Conversely, an effective writer may have difficulty reading, just as a tongue-tied person may be a great listener. The localization hypothesis helps explain these seemingly odd patterns of language control. It also suggests that each language function needs to be taught individually and be given sufficient classroom time and attention. To further your understanding of the localization theory, write an introspective essay focusing on your own proficiency in the four language skills. Are you equally proficient in all four skills, or do you tend to be more at ease with some rather than others?

2. Recent brain research has prompted language educators to explore so-called "brain-compatible" instructional approaches; that is, ways of teaching languages that are supported by findings in neurolinguistics. Brain research has confirmed the efficacy of techniques and strategies that teachers and caregivers have used, albeit intuitively, from time immemorial. Consider the instructional use of co-speech gestures in teaching. Nursery rhymes accompanied by finger play have been passed down from generation to generation. These days, educators have been experimenting with the use of finger play in teaching the entire range of language skills, including lexicon, pronunciation, and grammar. In one activity focused on the *is/are* distinction, the teacher encourages students to extend the index finger every time they use *is*, and to unfurl all four fingers when using *are*. The activity is effective because finger motions serve as visual representations of the verb form.

Develop similar activities. Identify a grammatical item that students find challenging (e.g., inverted verb order, or the ending -*s* in the third person singular) and develop co-speech gestures that could be used for practicing these language items. Develop a co-speech-gesture activity to teach writing conventions such as punctuation marks. Develop gestures that can be used to enhance comprehension of complex concepts, such as *gravity* and *electricity*.

WORDS TO REMEMBER

neurolinguistics: study of the brain control of language.

cortex: an outer sheet of brain cells that controls voluntary action, memory, language, and consciousness; also known as gray matter.

dichotic and dichoptic tests: testing procedures whereby two auditory or visual stimuli are presented simultaneously on the left and right side of the subject's body.

magnetic resonance imaging (MRI): a brain-imaging technique that shows the flow of blood to brain tissues.

positron emission tomography (PET): a brain-imaging technique that shows the flow of blood to brain tissues.

lesion: abnormal, damaged tissue.

aphasia: a total or partial loss of language.

Broca's area: the region of the brain involved in the production of fluent, well-formed speech.

Broca's aphasia: a loss of fluency and of the ability to produce well-formed utterances.

agrammatism: see **Broca's aphasia.**

circumlocution: elaborate, roundabout ways of saying things.

Wernicke's area: region of the brain involved in speech comprehension.

Wernicke's aphasia: a speech impairment resulting in an inability to comprehend or produce meaningful utterances.

flat affect: absence of emotional expressiveness.

lateralization: the functional specialization of one or the other brain hemisphere.

localization hypothesis: a theory according to which different brain areas are specialized for different functions.

declarative memory: long-term memory used for the retention of facts and events.

procedural memory: long-term memory used for learning motor skills.

mirror neurons: neurons that fire when an action is either performed or observed.

Notes

1. Obler, L., & Gjerlow, K. (1999). *Language and the brain.* New York: Cambridge University Press, p. 41.
2. Ibid., p. 43.
3. Sacks, O. (1986). *The man who mistook his wife for a hat.* South Yarmouth, MA: John Curley, p. 22.
4. Obler, L., & Gjerlow, K. (1999). *Language and the brain.* New York: Cambridge University Press.
5. Ross, E. D., & Monnot, M. (2008). Neurology of affective prosody and its functional-anatomic organization in the right hemisphere. *Brain and Language, 104*(1), 51–74.
6. Beeman, M. J., & Chiarello, C. (1998). Complementary right- and left-hemisphere language comprehension. *Current Directions in Psychological Science, 7*(1), 2–8.

7. Brownell, H. H., Simpson, T. L., Bihrle, A. M., Potter, H. H., & Gardner, H. (1990). Appreciation of metaphoric alternative word meanings by left and right brain-damaged patients. *Neuropsychologia*, *28*(4), 375–383.

8. Kim, H. S., Relkin, N. R., Lee, K.-M., & Hirsch, J. (1997). Distinct cortical areas associated with native and second languages. *Nature, 388*, 171–174.

9. Ullman, M. (2001). The neural basis of lexicon and grammar in first and second language: The declarative/procedural model. *Bilingualism: Language and Cognition, 4*(1), 105–122.

10. McNeill, D. (199). *Hand and mind: What gestures reveal about thought.* Chicago: University of Chicago Press.

11. Ibid.

12. Kendon, A. (1994). Do gestures communicate?: A review. *Research on Language and Social Interaction, 27*(3), 175–200.

13. Iverson, J. M., & Goldin-Meadow, S. (1997). What's communication got to do with it?: Gesture in children blind from birth. *Developmental Psychology, 33*, 453–467.

14. Rauscher, F. H., Krauss, R. M., & Chen, Y. (1996). Gesture, speech, and lexical access: The role of the lexical movements in speech production. *Psychological Science, 7*, 226–231.

15. Hadar, U., & Butterworth, B. (1997). Iconic gestures imagery and word retrieval in speech. *Semiotica, 115*, 147–172.

16. Klatzky, R. L., Pellegrino, J. W., McCloskey, B. P., & Doherty, S. (1989). Can you squeeze a tomato?: The role of motor representations in semantic sensibility judgments. *Journal of Memory and Language, 28*, 56–77.

17. Ravizza, S. (2003). Movement and lexical access: Do noniconic gestures aid in retrieval? *Psychonomic Bulletin and Review, 10*(3), 610–615.

18. Bates, E., & Dick, F. (2002). Language, gesture and the developing brain. *Developmental Psychology, 40*, 293–310.

19. Nicoladis, E., Mayberry, R. I., & Genessee, F. (1999). Gesture and early bilingual development. *Developmental Psychology, 35*(2), 514–526.

20. Kelly, S. D., Esch, M., & McDevitt, T. (2007). Neural correlates of learning Japanese words with or without iconic hand gesture. *Cognitive Neuroscience Abstracts B, 126*, 87.

21. Xu, J., Gannon, P. J., Emmorey, K., Smith, J. F., & Braun, A. R. (2009). Symbolic gestures and language are processed by a common neural system. *Proceedings of the National Academy of Sciences, 106*(49), 20664–20669.

22. Kelly, S. D., Manning, S. M., & Rodak, R. (2008). Gesture gives and hand to language and learning: Perspectives from cognitive neuroscience, developmental psychology and education. *Language and Linguistics Compass*, pp. 1–20.

23. Aziz-Zadeh L., Wilson S. M., Rizzolatti G., & Iacoboni, M. (2006). Congruent embodied representations for visually presented actions and linguistic phrases describing actions. *Current Biology, 16*(18), 1818–1823.

24. Nishitani, N., Schurmann, M., Amunts, K., & Hari, R. (2005). Broca's region: From action to language. *Physiology, 20*, 60–69.

7

First-Language Acquisition

Since ancient times, scientists have been intrigued by language learning in children. But recently, the Innateness Hypothesis has given special urgency to the study of first-language acquisition. Given that understanding the critical period may help unravel the mystery of innateness, numerous linguistic studies have focused on language learning in young children. What kind of predispositions enable children to master their mother tongue? Do children have language-learning abilities that adults lack? How early in the child's life are these abilities displayed? This chapter deals with some answers to these questions.

Before we discuss research findings, however, a few words are in order about the methods used for studying language development in young children and fetuses. That's right, fetuses! Scholars have even looked into fetuses' sensitivity to language. How do they do this?

One method, called *head-turn technique,* is based on the finding that when the fetus hears a new sound, it will turn its head toward the sound's source. When using head-turn technique, scientists create language stimuli around expectant women and observe the reaction of the fetus. Will the

The Educator's Guide to Linguistics, pages 93–108
Copyright © 2012 by Information Age Publishing
93

fetus turn its head or not? Another method is the *heart-deceleration technique*. When a fetus is exposed to a novel stimulus, its heart rate slows down. Given this reaction pattern, researchers present the fetus with language samples and watch to see if its heart rates decreases, the sign that it is taking notice.

When working with newborn babies, researchers use the so-called *high-amplitude sucking technique*. It is known that babies' sucking becomes more energetic and fast-paced when they hear something attention-worthy. So scientists attach a nipple to an electronic monitor, expose babies to verbal stimuli, and take notice of changes in their sucking patterns.

Early Sounds

Researchers used to believe that the only things the fetus is able to hear in utero are the flow of the mother's blood and her heartbeat. Recent studies, however, have demonstrated that the fetus can also hear his or her mother's voice. Researchers asked expectant mothers to say, "*Hello, baby. How are you today?*" Every time the mother spoke, the heart rate of the fetus slowed down. Apparently, the baby was able to discern the mother's voice and was paying attention![1]

Scientists also found that babies who are only a few days old can recognize their mother's voice and prefer it to the voices of other people.[2] Moreover, it was found that newborn babies recognize their mother tongue and prefer it to other languages. Spanish-speaking babies' sucking became much more enthusiastic when they heard Spanish than when they were exposed to English.[3]

An important study of infant phoneme perception has demonstrated that newborns are able to hear minute distinctions between the sounds of the world's languages. Researchers played a recording of the *ba* syllable to the newborns. At first, the babies showed interest by vigorously sucking on the nipple. Then the sucking rate slowed down. It was as if the babies said to themselves, "This is old hat!" When the researchers switched from *ba* to *pa*, however, the babies sucked with renewed vigor, an indication that they noticed the difference.[4] Significantly, only newborn babies can hear phonemic distinctions in a variety of the world's languages. As they grow up, children lose this ability and can only discriminate between the sounds of their mother tongue.[5] Apparently, young babies are primed to learn *any* language. They lose this special sensitivity, however, as they zero in on the language they are about to learn.

But how do babies learn to produce language sounds? Initially, the only noises babies make are those of crying, fretting, and burping. Around the age of 8 to 20 weeks, something new happens. One day, when the baby is content lying in her crib, she can be heard making soft, melodious noises: *ga-ga-ga*. This early vocalization, called *cooing*, consists of a consonant-like sound produced in the back of the throat, coupled with a vowel-like sound. Cooing is accompanied by tongue thrusting and lip movement—thought to be the baby's first efforts at imitating articulation. Around the time when they begin to coo, babies also produce their first hearty chuckles.

At around 25 to 50 weeks, babies reach another important milestone. One day, the baby says enthusiastically, *ba-ba-ba* or *da-da-da*. This vocalization is called babbling. First, babies do so-called *reduplicated babbling*, that is, repeating the same syllable over and over again. Later, babies move on to *variegated babbling*, in which they produce two different syllables (e.g., *da-ga, a-gu*).

Babies from different language backgrounds use a similar set of consonants when babbling. One study of 15 languages—including Mayan, Thai, Japanese, Hindi, Spanish, Arabic, and English—found that some sounds (e.g., *h, d, m,* and *t*) occurred with particular frequency. In addition, the study found that two sounds—*b* and *m*—were used by babies from all 15 language backgrounds.[6]

Interestingly enough, babies babble with the rhythm and intonation of their mother tongue. Some babies have veritable babbling conversations with themselves and others. The baby will ask a question, *Bababa?* and respond vigorously: *Bababa!* Intonational contours in babbling are such that adults are able to tell when babies are babbling in their own language. In one study, French-speaking adults were presented with samples of babbling produced by Arabic, Chinese, and French children. When babies kept babbling for a sufficiently long time, three-quarters of the informants were able to pick out the babbling of the French babies.[7]

At around the age of 13 to 18 months, the time when they begin to use words, babies produce the first actual vowels and consonants of their mother tongue. These early phonemes are imperfectly articulated and inconsistent in quality, with the final word sound often dropped, so that *gum* is pronounced "guh," and *nose* "no."

An interesting phenomenon in early language development is *reduplication*, that is, pronouncing the word's initial syllable twice. A little child may call the mouth *mamav*, money *mimi*, and the kitten *kiki*. Mostly, babies reduplicate two-syllable words, but monosyllabic ones can also be affected. For instance, one language learner called Christmas *didi*.[8] The role of reduplication in babies' speech is not clear. Some scientists believe that repeating a syllable gives babies an opportunity to play with sounds and practice their pronunciation. Others think that reduplication enables babies to master the overall syllabic structure of a word before they move on to its individual sounds.

It is interesting that, in many languages, infant words for male and female parents are made of reduplicated syllables. A study of kin terms in 474 languages revealed remarkable similarities between the English *mama* and *dada* and infant kin terms in other languages.[9]

Children are quick to learn some sounds (e.g., *m, p,* and *b*) and struggle with others (e.g., *l, r, sh*). That children have difficulty in pronouncing some sounds does not mean, however, that they are unable to hear the pronunciation nuances of their mother tongue. Children can actually distinguish between two similar sounds in a minimal pair. Here is one researcher's testimony:

> One of us [...] spoke to a child who called his inflated plastic fish a *fis*. In imitation of the child's pronunciation, the observer said: "This is your *fis*?" "No," said the child, "my *fis*." He continued to reject the adult's imitation until he was told, "That is your fish." "Yes," he said, "my fis."[10]

This quotation illustrates the pattern in first-language phonological development known as the *fis phenomenon*. This term refers to an asymmetry in the child's perception and production of language sounds. Even when children can distinguish between different sounds, they blur the distinction in their own speech. Here is an example of the fis phenomenon reported by another study:

> **Father:** Say "jump."
> **Child:** Dup.
> **Father:** No, "jump."
> **Child:** Dup.
> **Father:** No, "jummmp."
> **Child:** Only Daddy can say *dup!*[11]

Early Words

Children begin to produce their first words at around the age of 13 to 18 months. One day, the baby will see her father and excitedly say, *Dada! Dada!* Or, the baby will see a cookie and proclaim, *Caca!*

TABLE 7.1 Samples of Holophrases[12]

Utterance and context	Interpretation	Age (months)
Nana, in response to mother's "no"	I want to do that.	11
Ba(ll), having just thrown the ball	I'm throwing the ball.	11
Up, reaching up and in answer to "Do you want to get up?"	I want to get up.	13
Down, having just thrown something down	I am throwing it down.	14
Fishy, pointing to empty fish tank	The fish isn't there.	15

Often, early words are phrases that express statements or requests. *Dada!!*, for instance, may mean "Here is Daddy!" and *Caca!* may stand for "I want a cookie!". Because babies' first words are really sentences rolled into one word, linguists call them *holophrases*, or whole phrases. Table 7.1 provides some examples of holophrases and their interpretations.

Sometimes, toddlers pick up chunks of language, such as *gimme* ("give me"), *awgone* ("all gone"), or *wantit* ("I want it"), and use these multiword language pieces as single, unanalyzed units, without singling out individual words. Table 7.2 provides some more examples of such unsegmented language chunks.

Children seem to have two distinct word-learning styles. While some little language learners produce a lot of multiword chunks, which they pronounce rather unclearly, others prefer nouns, which they articulate clearly and carefully.

Some linguists believe that these two word-learning preferences reflect different cognitive styles. Users of language chunks seem to have more holistic learning styles and prefer to interact and express emotions. Noun us-

TABLE 7.2 Unsegmented Language Chunks in the Speech of Young Children[13]

Child's utterance	Meaning
Whasdat?	"What's that?"
Dunno	"I don't know."
Donwanna	"I don't want to."
Gimmedat	"Give me that."
Awgone	"All gone."
Lookadat	"Look at that."

ers, also called "patterners," are analytically minded. They like to name individual entities.[14]

In children, the process of word learning is inseparable from that of concept formation and is fraught with trial, error, and also linguistic creativity. Eighteen-month-old Sophie knew that a woolen hat she wore throughout the winter was topped with a *pompom*. One spring day, Sophie's mother brought a plateful of strawberries into the room and set it on the table. Upon contemplating this glorious sight, Sophie jubilantly exclaimed, *Pompom!* Here, the child applied the familiar label where it did not belong. This naming strategy is called *overextension*.[15]

Overextension is an example of children's ingenious way with language. It is if the child reasoned, "I don't know what this thing is called, but it looks like something I know quite well. So I am just going to use the word I know for this new thing." Children overextend when there is a perceptual similarity or semblance between two objects or when the two objects have similar functions. For instance, one baby called all birds and insects *quack* because they all have wings and fly. Upon noting an eagle on the face of a coin, this baby dubbed the coin *quack*. Another, mechanically inclined language learner called various gadgets *tick tocks*. In this young language learner's view, clocks, a gas-meter, a fire hose on a spool, and a scale with a round dial were all different kinds of *tick tocks*. Table 7.3 shows some other examples of overextensions.

Young children are adept at coining new words. Often, when a little language learner needs to name something and does not have a word readily available, she proceeds to create her own label.

When coining new words, children display intuitive understanding of their mother tongue's morphology. In Chapter 3, you learned about compounding and derivation, two mechanisms that speakers use for coining words.

Children are confident users of these word-formation strategies. They use derivations, such as *lessoner* ("teacher"), *braker* ("car brake"), and com-

TABLE 7.3   Examples of Overextensions[16]

Word	First referent	Extension
candy	candy	cherries, anything sweet
apple	apples	balls, tomatoes, cherries, onions, biscuits
turtle	turtles	fish, seals
kitty	cats	rabbits, any small furry animal

pounds, such as *fix-man* ("mechanic"). At supper, a mother teasingly asked her 2-year-old, *Are you an eye-blinker?* The child clapped her hands and said, *I am a clapper.* When getting out of the car, the same toddler announced, *I am going to shut the door hard because I am a shutter.* When playing with a mug, she said, *I have a sip. I am a sipper.*[17]

English is distinct from many other languages in that, in English, the noun can be turned into a verb or an adjective, depending on its position in the sentence. (For instance, the noun *hand* becomes a verb in the sentence *Can you hand me the napkin?.*)

Children who learn English as their mother tongue are virtuoso creators of such noun-based verbs called *denominal verbs. And did you needle this?* inquired a child of her mother who was mending socks. *But I did not blade myself!* said another one reassuringly when picking up a Cuisinart blade from the sink. *How do you know where to . . . to scissor?* asked a child looking at a carton of apple juice that the adult was about to open. *And it will wind all the toys away,* said another child on a windy day.[18]

Children's word development undergoes a dramatic change when they reach the age of 2. Before their second birthday, toddlers' vocabularies number a few dozen words. After this milestone, however, infants' word power grows immensely. During the period of vocabulary expansion (referred to as the *vocabulary burst, naming explosion,* or *word spurt*), some children learn up to 10 words a week. The vocabulary burst goes on through the preschool, kindergarten, and elementary-school years. It has been estimated that, during some particularly intense periods of word learning, children memorize up to 10 words a day. (Take a foreign-language dictionary, jot down 10 new words, and try to memorize them. This little exercise, which most adults find extremely challenging, might give you some idea of the magnitude of the task that children perform quite effortlessly.)

The vocabulary burst is particularly remarkable, given that children don't get any help with their word learning. Adults very infrequently take the time to explain to a child what this or that word means. Children simply pick up new words from their environment.

Sometimes the child will play around adults, seemingly without paying attention to their conversation. Then, immediately following this situation, or even several days later, the child will use a new word. Apparently, the child overheard the word, figured out what it meant, and remembered it, too.

What kinds of processes are involved in this type of word learning? A study of the acquisition of color terms by young children provides some insight.[19] Researchers conducted an experiment where they asked 3- to 4-year-old children to give them a block. When children gave researchers a green block, adults said, *No. Not the green one, give me the chromium one.* Using context alone, children inferred that the word *chromium* referred to the color of the blocks in the other tray and handed the correct block to the researchers. Perhaps most impressively, even one week after hearing the word *chromium,* children still remembered the new word. The ability to learn the word after one brief exposure is known as *fast mapping.*

Learning Grammar

The toddler's first sentence may be *Mommy sock* or *Sit lap!* Made of two words and lacking grammatical elements, these utternaces are known as telegraphic speech. Just like the brief messages that were once sent by telegraph, these early sentences lack auxiliaries, prepositions, and other functional elements.

Table 7.4 provides samples of telegraphic sentences produced by a baby named Jeff.

When children do begin to use grammatical elements, they do not just copy adult sentences. A distinct feature of children's grammar learning is creativity. While learning first-language grammar, children unpack or analyze the language they hear, infer and internalize grammatical rules, and then proceed to apply them. A famous test performed by linguist Jean Berko demonstrates this process.[21] In Berko's experiment, which came to be known as the *wug test,* young children were presented with a picture of an imaginary birdlike creature and were told that the creature was called a *wug* (Figure 7.1). Then Berko presented the subjects with another pic-

TABLE 7.4　Samples of Telegraphic Speech Produced by Young Children.[20]

Two-word sentence	Possible meaning
Mommy sock.	"That's Mommy's sock." "Mommy, put on my sock."
More juice!	"I want more juice."
Allgone outside!	"The outside is all gone" (said after the front door is closed).
Throw chicken.	"[Dad] is throwing the [toy] chicken."
Car go.	"The car is going."
Sweater chair.	"The sweater is on the chair."
Little dog.	"The dog is little."
That Susan.	"That is Susan." "Her name is Susan."

THIS IS A WUG.

NOW THERE IS ANOTHER ONE.

THERE ARE TWO OF THEM.

THERE ARE TWO _____.

Figure 7.1   Pictures used in the wug test.

ture and said, *Now there is another one. There are two of them. Now there are two* _____*? *The children reacted by saying, *two wugs*. The test demonstrates that children are able to produce forms they have not heard before.

Young children can be heard to exclaim, *Look what I bringed!* and to ask, *Why did you did it?* This pattern of language use is called *overgeneralization*. When children overgeneralize, they do use a rule of English grammar. However, they use a grammatical form where it does not really belong.

Children first master irregular forms (e.g., *feet, brought*) and then the regular ones (e.g., *cats, lived*). Interestingly, at the time when children first begin using regular forms (e.g., the *-s* and *-ed* endings), they stop using irregulars—albeit temporarily—and apply regular endings indiscriminately. It is at this point that children can be heard saying *feets* and *bringed*. However, once the regular forms have been properly mastered, children stop overgeneralizing and go back to the correct use of irregular forms.[22]

But which grammatical forms do children master first? Which ones come second? Psychologist Roger Brown conducted a study involving three toddlers: Adam, Eve, and Sara. Brown's study demonstrated that all three children learned their morphemes in the same order as follows:

Step 1. *-ing*
Steps 2–3. *in* and *on*
Step 4. plural *-s*
Step 5. irregular past of the verb (e.g., *pulled*)
Step 6. possessive *-'s* (e.g., *mom's*)
Step 7. uncontractible copula (e.g., *Who is sick? He is.*)
Step 8. *the, a*
Step 9. regular past tense *-ed*
Step 10. third-person singular *-s* (e.g., *works*)
Step 11. third-person irregular (e.g., *does, has*)
Step 12. uncontractible auxiliary *be* (*Who is wearing your hat? He is.*)
Step 13. contractible copula (e.g., *He's big.*)
Step 14. contractible auxiliary (*Daddy's eating.*)[23]

Brown also found that the rate at which the three children learned to speak did not impact the order of acquisition. The more verbal Eve moved through her grammar-learning stages a little faster than Adam or Sara. What really matters is that all three subjects followed the same steps in the same order.

Experiments like the one conducted by Brown are called *morpheme-order studies*. They have all provided similar evidence: Children learn grammar in fixed steps that instruction is powerless to change.

What is the significance of these findings? Why are morpheme-order studies undertaken in the first place? In the first chapter of this book, you read that innate skills are learned in a predetermined order. If innatists are right, and grammar is indeed wired into our genes, it would stand to reason to hypothesize that children learn grammar following a predetermined sequence. This is exactly what morpheme-order studies have demonstrated, providing additional evidence in support of innateness and the Universal Grammar hypothesis. The fixed route for language development has been dubbed the *innate syllabus*.

That said, not all researchers find the evidence from morpheme-order studies compelling. Some say that English morphemes are learned in a particular order because certain morphemes have greater *perceptual saliency* and are more likely to catch children's attention. According to this argument, the bound morpheme *-ing* is learned first because it crops up a lot in the speech of adults, who tend to say things like *What is daddy doing?* or *Look at the birdie. The birdie is flying* when talking to toddlers.

There are also linguists who feel there is a need for additional morpheme-order studies of children from different language backgrounds before definitive conclusions can be reached.

The Role of Caretakers

Children do seem to have unique abilities for language learning. They are able to hear minute differences between language sounds, coin new words, remember dozens of new labels, and discover rules of grammar. But what *is* the role of adults in children's language development?

It is commonly held that adults "teach" babies how to speak. This, however, is not the case. Of course, adults do teach children some new words. But, as you know, children pick up most words simply by being exposed to them.

Nor do adults teach little children how to speak grammatically. Careful observation of parents has demonstrated that, while mothers tend to correct factual mistakes made by their children, they usually ignore their mistakes with grammar. Moreover, mothers often repeat endearing ungrammatical forms produced by their offspring.[24]

In the rare instances when adults do correct children's grammar, their corrections do not make much of a difference. More often than not, children simply ignore adult negative feedback. The dialogue below is a case in point:

Child: My teacher holded the baby rabbits and we patted them.
Adult: Did you say your teacher held the baby rabbits?
Child: Yes.
Adult: What did you say she did?
Child: She holded the baby rabbits and we patted them.
Adult: Did you say she held them tightly?
Child: No, she holded them loosely.[25]

Even when adults perform so-called *recasts* (modeling the correct form and encouraging the child to repeat the model), *children are unable to imitate the correct pattern.* Consider the following examples of failed recasts:

Example 1:
Child: Nobody don't like me.
Mother: No, say "nobody likes me."

> **Child:** Nobody don't like me.
>
> *[Eight repetitions of this dialogue]*
>
> **Mother:** No, now listen carefully; say "Nobody likes me."
>
> **Child:** Oh! Nobody don't like*s* me.[26]

Example 2:

> **Child:** Want other one spoon, daddy.
>
> **Father:** You mean, you want the other spoon.
>
> **Child:** Yes, I want other one spoon, please Daddy.
>
> **Father:** Can you say "the other spoon"?
>
> **Child:** Other . . . one . . . spoon.
>
> **Father:** Say "other."
>
> **Child:** Other.
>
> **Father:** Spoon.
>
> **Child:** Spoon.
>
> **Father:** Other spoon.
>
> **Child:** Other . . . spoon. Now give me other one spoon.[27]

These interactions are by no means unusual. Numerous studies suggest that children are able to repeat grammatical models only when they are already on the brink of mastering the form in question and are beginning to produce it on their own.

The bottom line is that children discover grammar on their own. They do so by following what may be the innate syllabus—which adult corrections seem powerless to change.

But are there strategies that adults can use to enhance language acquisition in children? Such strategies do exist and are used, albeit intuitively, by many caretakers.

Take *motherese*, or *baby talk* or *infant-directed speech*, a language form that adults use when interacting with babies and toddlers. The distinguishing features of motherese are a higher-than-normal pitch and greater-than-normal pitch range; a slow speech tempo; exaggerated, elongated vowels and exaggerated intonation (e.g., *Good moooorning!*); short, repetitive, simple sentence frames (e.g., *Where is Sammy? Here he is! Where is Mommy? Here she is!*); frequent commands and questions (e.g., *Do sooo big! Say "bye-bye"! What does doggie say?*); simplified, often reduplicated words (e.g., *choo-choo train, bye-bye*), and words with diminutive endings (e.g., *doggie, horsie*). There is strong research evidence that babies respond well to motherese, and that it is beneficial for their language development.

Roberta Golinkoff, an expert in early language acquisition, cites a study of teenage mothers interacting with their babies. Perhaps because they were themselves not far removed in age from their children, and were self-conscious about using baby talk, young mothers were found to be silent when taking care of their babies. This conspicuous absence of motherese resulted in delays in their infants' language development.[28]

Motherese is not, however, crucial for language learning. In some cultures, adults do not use baby talk and do not adapt their speech in any way when talking to children.[29] Even so, children from those cultures learn to speak their mother tongue.

The one factor that is absolutely critical for the child's language development to be triggered is the availability of speech that a child can comprehend. If the language to which the child is exposed is not elucidated by either context or interaction or both, language learning is not going to take place. This is why hearing children of deaf parents do not pick up language from mere exposure to television or radio. However, if children comprehend the language they hear, they will inevitably pick it up.

Implications for Instruction

1. The finding that first-language development occurs in preordained sequences has important instructional implications. Understanding what a child can (and cannot) do at a certain age is crucial for designing the optimal language-teaching curriculum and will save the teacher many uphill battles. We can learn a great deal about the stages and constraints involved in language maturation by observing children. What patterns of language use does the child display? What type of language does he or she respond to?

   Conduct a mini-study of a child's pattern of language use at a given age.

2. Some of the more effective classroom activities tap into children's creativity with language. In one lesson, children describe an imaginary island they have "discovered"; the students label the mountains, lakes, plains, and rivers found on their island. In another activity, students create a creature from outer space that speaks its own extraterrestrial language. In this activity, the teacher encourages children to make a list of words and phrases

used by the imaginary out-of-space visitor. Create a similar activity that capitalizes on children's linguistic creativity.

3. Jokes, riddles, and chants that accompany games are enjoyed by children throughout the world. Poems such as "I was going to Kentucky," "Miss Lucy had a baby," and numerous other energy-filled, rhythmic texts have been passed down from generation to generation, because they satisfy children's need to play with language. Playground poems have enormous instructional potential. For instance, young children can recite the "The Itsy Bitsy Spider" poem and create their own stories describing the adventures of a traveling bug. Collect samples of texts recited by children when they play at home or on the playground. Analyze the structure of these texts. Create activities based on these texts.

WORDS TO REMEMBER

head-turn technique, heart-rate deceleration technique, high-amplitude sucking technique: research methods used to study language perception in fetuses and infants.

cooing: early vocalization made of strings of back-throat consonants and vowels.

babbling: early vocalization consisting of consonants and vowels.

reduplicated babbling: repeating the same syllable in babbling.

variegated babbling: producing a variety of syllables in babbling.

phonological reduplication: repeating the first syllable of a word.

fis phenomenon: infants' ability to recognize sounds they are unable to produce.

holophrases: single-word utterances produced by young children.

overextension: in children's speech, applying a familiar word to new referents.

denominal verbs: verbs derived from nouns.

vocabulary burst, naming explosion, word spurt: three names for a stage of intense word learning in young children.

fast mapping: learning word meaning after a single brief exposure.

telegraphic speech: early sentences lacking grammatical elements.

morpheme-order studies: studies that investigate the sequences of grammatical maturation.

innate syllabus: the predetermined order for acquiring grammatical forms; believed to be impervious to instruction.

perceptual salience: quality of a linguistic item that makes that item likely to draw attention.

wug test: the experiment that demonstrates that children produce grammatical forms they have not heard.

overgeneralization: applying a grammatical form where it does not belong.

recast: responding to an error by repeating the utterance with the error corrected.

motherese, caretaker speech, baby talk: three names for a form of speech used by adults when talking to infants.

Notes

1. Feifer, W. P., & Moon, C. (1988). Auditory experience in the fetus. In W. P. Smotherman & S. R. Robinson (Eds.), *Behavior of the fetus* (pp. 175–188) Caldwell, NJ: Telford Press.
2. DeCasper, A. J., & Fifer, M. J. (1980). On human bonding: Newborns prefer their mothers' voices. *Science, 208,* 1174–1176.
3. Moon, C., Cooper, R., & Fifer, W. (1993). Two-day-olds prefer their native language. *Infant Behavior and Development, 16,* 495–500.
4. Eimas, P., Siqueland, E., Jusczyk, P., & Vigorito, J. (1971). Speech perception in infants. *Science, 171,* 303–306.
5. Werker, J., & Tees, R. (1983). Developmental changes across childhood in the perception of non-native speech sounds. *Canadian Journal of Psychology, 37*(2), 278–286.
6. Locke, J. (1983). *Phonological acquisition and change.* New York: Academic Press, pp. 9–11.
7. de Boysson-Bardies, B., Sagart, L., & Durand, C. (1984). Discernable differences in the babbling of infants according to target language. *Journal of Child Language, 11,* 1–16.
8. Schwartz, R., Leonard, L., Wilcox, M. J., & Folger, M. K. (1980). Again and again: Reduplication in child phonology. *Journal of Child Language, 7,* 75–87.
9. Murdock, G. (1959). Cross-language parallels in parental kin terms. *Anthropological Linguistics, 1*(9), 1–5.
10. Berko, J., & Brown, R. (1960). Psycholinguistic research methods. In P. Mussen (Ed.), *Handbook of research methods in child development* (pp. 517–557). New York: Wiley.
11. Smith, N. (1973). *The acquisition of phonology: A case study.* London: Cambridge University Press, p. 10.
12. Adapted from Greenfield, P., & Smith, J. (1976). *The structure of communication in early language development.* New York: Academic Press, p. 70.

13. O'Grady, W. (2005). *How children learn language.* Cambridge, UK: Cambridge University Press, p. 11.
14. Nelson, K. (1981). Individual differences in language development: Implications for development and learning. *Developmental Psychology, 17*(2), 170–187.
15. Eydinov, S. Personal communication.
16. O'Grady, W. (2005). *How children learn language.* Cambridge, UK: Cambridge University Press, p. 46.
17. Clark, E. (2003). *First language acquisition.* Cambridge, UK: Cambridge University Press, p. 290.
18. Adapted from Clark, E. (1993). *The lexicon in acquisition.* New York: Cambridge University Press, p. 200.
19. Carey, S., & Bartlett, E. (1978). Acquiring a single new word. *Papers and Reports on Child Language Development, 15,* 17–29.
20. Golinkoff, R., & Hirsh-Pasek, K. (1999). *How babies talk: The magic and mystery of language in the first three years of life.* New York: Penguin Books, p. 151.
21. Berko, J. (1958). The child's learning of English morphology. *Word, 14,* 150–177.
22. Marcus, G. F., Pinker, S., Ullman, M., Hollander, M., Rosen, T. J., & Xu, F. (1992). Overregularization in language acquisition. *Monographs of the Society for Research in Child Development, 57*(4).
23. Adapted from Brown, R. (1973). *A first language: The early stages.* Cambridge, MA: Harvard University Press, p. 274.
24. Hirsh-Pasek, K., Treiman, R., & Schneiderman, M. (1984). Brown & Hanlon revisited: Mothers' sensitivity to ungrammatical forms. *Journal of Child Language, 11,* 81–88.
25. Gleason, J. B. (1967). Do children imitate? Paper presented at the International Conference on Oral Education of the Deaf, Lexington School for the Deaf, New York. Cited in Cazden, C. (1972). *Child language and education.* New York: Holt, Rinehart & Winston, p. 92.
26. McNeill, D. (1966). Developmental psycholinguistics. In F. Smith & G. Miller (Eds.), *The genesis of language: A psycholinguistic approach* (pp. 15–84). Cambridge, MA: MIT Press, p. 69.
27. Braine, M. (1971). On two types of models of the internalization of grammars. In D. I. Slobin (Ed.), *The ontogenesis of grammar: A theoretical symposium* (pp. 153–186). New York: Academic Press.
28. Golinkoff, R., & Hirsh-Pasek, K. (1999). *How babies talk: The magic and mystery of language in the first three years of life.* New York: Penguin Books.
29. Lieven, E. (1994). Crosslinguistic and crosscultural aspects of language addressed to children. In C. Gallaway & B. Richards (Eds.), *Input and interaction in language acquisition* (pp. 56–73). New York: Cambridge University Press.

8

Second-Language Acquisition

This chapter deals with second-language acquisition, or *SLA* for short. SLA studies examine the process of learning *L2* or the *target language*, a language other than one's mother tongue. (The mother tongue is known as "L1.") SLA research distinguishes between two kinds of L2s: second languages and foreign languages. A second language is one acquired over an extended time period, usually in a situation of total immersion. An immigrant, for instance, learns a second language. A foreign language, in contrast, is studied within the limited timeframe of formal schooling.

Of special interest to teachers is L2 learning in children. Are children more successful language learners than adults? How do young students master L2 grammar? How do they develop target language vocabulary? Chapter 8 addresses these questions. It is primarily concerned with second-language learning.

The Silent Period and the Rejection Period

When they first find themselves in situations of L2 immersion, most young learners go through a *silent period*, a stage when they make no attempt to use

The Educator's Guide to Linguistics, pages 109–125
Copyright © 2012 by Information Age Publishing
All rights of reproduction in any form reserved.

the new language. The duration of this period varies. Some children will start speaking L2 after just a few weeks; it takes others up to several months or even a year before they are ready to utter their first L2 words. Here is how one Korean American described her silent period:

> I had spent kindergarten in almost complete silence, hearing only the high nasality of my teacher and comprehending little but the cranky wails and cries of my classmates.[1]

The silent period is by no means unproductive, though. During this stage, children become sensitized to L2 sounds and grammar, develop initial comprehension skills, and learn their first L2 words.

In a few rare instances, young second-language learners go through a *rejection period*, a phase of extremely adverse reaction to the new language. These children become morose and shun interaction with L2 speakers. One study has described a Japanese child who, during his first months in an American nursery school, spent most of his time on a tricycle as far as possible from the other children, especially those who spoke English. Every time the observer addressed the boy in English, "he ignored her, turned away, or ran out of the room."[2]

Language Transfer and Contrastive Analysis

Language transfer is applying the skills from L1 when learning the target language. If the target language and the home language have a feature in common, the transfer is positive. For instance, *cognates*, or words of similar origin, help learners learn target language words. Thus, a French-speaking student of English is likely to find hundreds of English words easy to learn because English has numerous French cognates (e.g., *chair/chaise, abandon/abandonner, difficult/difficile*).

But language transfer can also be negative. *Negative transfer* takes place when first-language skills interfere with target-language learning. For instance, because many languages lack the interdental sounds, speakers of those languages realize *This Thursday* as "dis Tursday." Similarly, since Chinese nouns do not have past-tense markers, a Chinese-speaking learners of English tend to have difficulty learning the English past-tense marker *-ed*. Or because in Spanish the adjective follows a noun (e.g., *camisa blanca*), speakers of Spanish may use an adjective in a postposition when learning English, producing forms such as **shirt white*.[3]

In the 1970s, during the early stages of SLA research, linguists used a procedure called *contrastive analysis*. Contrastive analysis involves identifying errors due to structural mismatches between L1 and L2 and developing a syllabus to prevent those errors. According to this model, teaching L2 should be, first and foremost, concerned with preventing errors caused by negative transfer.

However, when linguists applied contrastive analysis to language teaching, they were met with a surprise. The data suggested that, while contrastive analysis was effective in accounting for phonological errors or a foreign accent, it was less helpful in predicting grammatical errors.

SLA studies suggest that, initially at least, language learners do make errors due to first-language negative transfer. Thus, as predicted by contrastive analysis, speakers of Chinese produce phrases such as *I work yesterday* and speakers of Spanish say, for instance, *they have hungry* (because of influence from the Spanish *ellos tienen hambre*). However, as the learner's proficiency grows, errors due to negative transfer begin to fade away.[4]

What sort of errors *cannot* be accounted by the transfer of L1 skills? Let us consider some examples. When speakers of Norwegian ask a question, they invert the order of subject and verb, placing the verb before the subject. If the rules of negative transfer held, Norwegian children learning to speak English would transpose the verb and the noun and say, *Where drink you?* However, Rune and Reidun, two Norwegian-speaking children learning to speak English, used the same word order as their English-speaking peers. When asking questions, Rune and Reidun produced sentences, such as *What you drink?* and *What dem [them] eating?*[5] Or take another example. In Japanese, the negative particle is placed after the verb. Thus, one might expect that a Japanese-speaking child learning English would say, *I like no*. However, Ken, a 7-year-old Japanese boy, produced patterns similar to those used by his English-speaking peers (e.g., *Me no win*, *I no like small*).[6] Errors of this kind are developmental; they are made by *all* young English language learners.

Today, linguists distinguish between *interlingual* and *intralingual errors*. Interlingual errors are made because of divergences between L1 and L2 structures. Intralingual errors are made by all L2 learners, irrespective of their first language.[7]

Creative Construction and Interlanguage

Consider some more utterances produced by young ESL students: *I garbaged my paper. *I were doing it first! *This block is mines. These errors are not random slips. They suggest mental effort to make sense of language data. Take the utterance *This block is mines*. If we could unravel the mental process leading to this pattern, it would be something like this: "People say *hers*, *his*, *theirs*, and *ours*. *Mines* has got to be right, because, like the other ones, it ends in -*s*."

The errors just mentioned are a product of an active (albeit unconscious) mental process known as *creative construction*. When engaging in creative construction, learners analyze L2 in their environment and develop hypotheses about its structure.

To refer to a language form resulting from creative construction, linguists use the term *interlanguage*.[8] Interlanguage is an approximation of L2, an idiom used by learners on their way to L2 proficiency. Interlanguage is an evolving system. Learners continually revise their hypotheses with relation to L2 structures and adjust their interlanguages accordingly.

Morpheme-Order Studies

What are the stages of interlanguage development? The sequences in which grammar is learned are explored in so-called *morpheme-order studies*.

An important morpheme-order study deals with young Spanish- and Chinese-speaking learners of English.[9] This study suggests that all children, no matter what their first language, learn English bound morphemes in the same order, as follows:

1. plural -*s*
2. progressive -*ing*
3. copula *be* (e.g., *This game is fun.*)
4. auxiliary *be* (e.g., *They are playing.*)
5. the definite and indefinite articles *the* and *a*
6. irregular past tenses
7. third-person singular ending -*s*
8. possessive ending -*s* (e.g., *My mom's picture*).

Researchers have been particularly impressed by the finding that acquisition orders seem to be the same in speakers of languages as vastly different from each other as Spanish and Chinese. Chinese, for instance, does not have a copula analogous to the English *be* or the Spanish *ser* and *estar*. Yet both Chinese- and Spanish-speaking subjects acquired the copula at the same stage. Similarly, even though Spanish forms plurals in the same way that English does, Chinese-speaking children mastered this feature at the same stage as their Spanish-speaking peers. The rate of acquisition varies from child to child. What matters, though, is that the acquisition sequences seem to be preordained, and that instruction is powerless to change them.

What is to be made of these findings? Some researchers argue that they provide another piece of evidence that our language ability is biologically determined. (After all, as you may recall, innate behaviors are learned according to a rigid schedule.) Other researchers contend that the question of whether there is a congenital syllabus for grammar remains open, and that it will require future studies to demonstrate that the grammar sets of all L2s are learned in a fixed order.

At the same time, there are scholars who argue that the fixed order of morpheme acquisition is unrelated to innateness. They believe that certain L2 structures are learned ahead of others because they are more likely to catch learners' attention. According to this position, the order of morpheme acquisition has to do with some forms' greater *perceptual saliency*.

Ultimate Attainment

Does research bear out the popular belief that children are more adept L2 learners than adults? There is no straightforward answer to this question. Studies suggest that, during the early stages of language learning, little children may lag behind adults.[10] There is evidence, for instance, that adult learners initially have less difficulty in learning grammar.[11]

As time goes on, however, young children make increasingly greater strides with language learning, eventually outpacing grownups. Early learners—that is, people who learned L2 during childhood—may not necessarily enjoy advanced literacy skills, sophisticated L2 vocabulary, or knowledge of prescriptive grammar rules. It is significant, though, that they all develop native-like fluency. It is usually impossible or next to impossible to tell an early language learner from a native speaker. Linguists say that children's *ultimate attainment* is superior to that of adults.[12]

Early learners' superior ultimate attainment is particularly evident in phonology. Whereas most adult learners keep a foreign accent, young language learners develop native-like pronunciation. A study comparing two groups of immigrants—those who came to the United States in childhood and those who immigrated in adulthood—demonstrated that age of arrival, rather than duration of stay in the United States, was the factor that determined whether a language learner lost or retained a foreign accent. Those subjects who were children when they came to the United States sounded like native-born Americans.[13]

Is there a window of opportunity for native-like ultimate attainment? While the evidence is inconclusive,[14] many linguists believe that the cutoff age is puberty. The prepubescent period conducive to native-like L2 attainment is known as the *sensitive period.*

Linguistic Intuition

What are the limitations displayed by adult L2 learners? Take the phrase *I have great excitement to receive your email.* It is free of errors. Most native speakers would agree, however, that it is awkward and that they would not use it. Native speakers' intuitive knowledge of whether a language pattern is acceptable or not is called *linguistic intuition.* Native speakers are not necessarily able to explain why they find a certain pattern jarring and another one acceptable. Significantly, though, their judgments of acceptability seldom diverge. This kind of instinctive linguistic knowledge is different from knowledge of prescriptive grammar, acquired consciously during the years of formal schooling.

Some SLA studies have investigated linguistic intuition. For instance, studies of *grammaticality judgment* focus on learners' ability to determine whether a phrase is well formed or ill formed, that is, whether its grammatical structure is or isn't native-like.

Studies have demonstrated that early and late learners perform differently on grammaticality judgment tasks.[15] Researchers worked with 46 native speakers of Chinese and Korean who arrived in the United States between the ages of 3 and 39 and had lived in the United States between 3 and 26 years. The subjects were asked to pick well-formed sentences from pairs such as *The little boy is speaking to a policeman* and **The little boy is speak to a policeman,* or *Tom is reading a book in the bathtub* and **Tom is reading book in the bathtub.* The study demonstrated that early arrivals consistently did better than late arrivals on grammaticality-judgment tasks. The cutoff age was puberty. Early learners' grammaticality judgment was native-like. However, if subjects started learning English after puberty, their grammaticality judgment was erratic and inconsistent.

Fossilization

Another limitation that is only observed in late L2 learners is *fossilization.* Coined by American linguist Larry Selinker, the term "fossilization" refers to a non-native feature in learner speech that no amount of instruction can eliminate.[16]

Fossilization may follow two patterns. Sometimes, learners reach a plateau, getting "stuck" at an early proficiency level and ceasing to make any further progress. In other cases, even though learners' proficiency keeps growing, they fail to master some select L2 items.

If you know an English-language-learner who says, **Thanks God!*, or **commit a suicide*, or **I live in the U.S. for 10 years*, even though you have gently suggested a number of times that the correct forms are actually *Thank God!*, *commit suicide*, and *I have lived in the U.S. for ten years*, then you are dealing with cases of item-specific fossilization.

Fundamental Difference Hypothesis

The important findings just discussed have given rise to the *fundamental difference hypothesis*; that is, the belief that language-learning processes work differently in adults and children. Robert Bley-Vroman, a theorist behind this position, argues that, because young language learners still have access to their Universal Grammar (UG), they acquire L2 instinctively. In contrast, adults, whose UG is no longer active, rely on common reasoning skills when learning L2.[17]

Consider your own L2 learning experience. If you studied a second or foreign language after puberty, you may recall going over grammar rules or foreign words in your mind and making conscious decisions about which one to use. This conscious linguistic decision making is an example of using the common reasoning skills referred to by Bley-Vroman. But maybe you learned another language at a young age. If that is the case, it is unlikely that you consciously monitored your own speech. Most probably, you just picked up pieces of language from your teachers and your peers and instinctively used them in sentences. Proponents of the Fundamental Difference Hypothesis argue that these profoundly different learning styles have to do with learner ability to tap into UG, or lack thereof.

L2 Teaching Methodology

A few words are in order about L2 teaching methodology, the discipline that investigates ways of teaching L2. While discussing past and recent trends in L2 teaching, we pay special attention to the controversy surrounding grammar instruction. The grammar debate deserves special attention because schools of methodology have been largely defined by how they have dealt with the question of whether and how grammar needs to be taught.

The *grammar-translation method*, one of the first coherent systems of language teaching, was derived from the 19th-century approach to teach students to read and write in Greek and Latin. This method emphasized grammar instruction. In the grammar-translation classroom, students studied L2 grammar rules, memorized words, and then practiced translating sentences from L2 into L1. As a result, learners developed literacy skills but did not become fluent in L2.

The late 19th century was a time of growing affluence in the United States. The Gilded Age gave Americans an appetite for travel and an interest in learning to speak foreign languages. It was at this time that linguist Maximilian Berlitz (whose name the famous chain of language schools bears to this day) developed the *direct method* of foreign-language teaching. This method was based on the theoretical assumption that adults learn a foreign language similarly to the way children learn their mother tongue. In the direct method classroom, the teacher and students only use L2. Translating into students' home languages is avoided. While presenting students with increasingly complex phrases, the teacher clarifies their meaning by elaborate pantomime and gestures. Grammar rules are not taught explicitly. Instead, students are expected to infer them from teacher speech. The direct method has major limitations. For instance, it relies on time-consuming clarification techniques where a translation would have worked much more efficiently. Also questionable is the direct method's theoretical premise that equates L2 learning in adults with native-language learning in children.

In the 1950s, the educational agenda in the United States was shaped by the Cold War with the Communist Bloc. U.S. political leaders, concerned with making the country's system of education more competitive, charged educators with the task of developing truly effective, research-based language-teaching methods. The *audiolingual method* developed during this time was informed by behaviorist psychology's tenet that learning is underpinned by habit formation. To reinforce the use of correct L2 forms, the audio-lingiual instruction used drills that were performed in audio-lingual labs. Since the method emphasized mastery of grammar, students practiced sentences that highlighted various L2 grammar points. While learners who performed lab drills ended up memorizing a lot of sentences, they never learned to use L2 spontaneously.

In the 1960s, Chomsky and his followers leveled harsh criticism against the audiolingual method. Innatists argued that linguistic competence draws on UG, an innate body of intuitive grammatical knowledge that enables speakers to form an infinite number of new sentences. Because language ability is inherently creative—went the innatist argument—language cannot possibly be learned by imitation. Cognitive code, the school of language teaching informed by innatist theories, placed emphasis on teaching grammar.

The *communicative approach* emerged in the 1970s as a reaction against the Chomskyan linguistic theory. Proponents of the communicative approach have argued that the innatist model overlooked two aspects of language: its formulaic nature and its link to the culture. According to this view, *communicative competence*—that is, L2 proficiency—has a lot to do with learner ability to use set expressions in day-to-day situations, following the cultural conventions. The communicative approach utilizes interactive activities such as role-plays and dialogues. It does include some grammar instruction, but only insofar as it serves learners' communicative needs. For instance, students practice the *I am going to have* _____ pattern when learning how to order food in a restaurant. While this approach is effective for developing basic communication skills, it does not necessarily ensure advanced L2 proficiency.

Arguably the most influential theory of language learning and teaching to emerge in recent years is the *Natural Approach*. Developed in the 1980s by Stephen Krashen, the Natural Approach is based on five underlying hypotheses:

1. *The language learning versus language acquisition hypothesis.* According to this hypothesis, there is a difference between language acquisition and language learning. While acquisition is an unconscious process of picking up L2, learning is a process of conscious and formal L2 study. Only language acquisition leads to true competence.

2. *The monitor hypothesis.* This proposition holds that using monitoring, or consciously checking one's speech for errors, is part of language learning, not language acquisition. The Natural Approach is critical of monitoring because it allegedly inhibits language production.

3. *The natural order hypothesis.* This is the claim that grammatical structures are acquired in a predictable order that instruction is powerless to change.

4. *The comprehensible input hypothesis.* This theory states that learners acquire L2 best when they are exposed to messages slightly above their proficiency levels. Thus, the optimal situation for L2 acquisition is one in which the learner understands what is being said and also encounters some new target-language items.

5. *The affective filter hypothesis.* According to this view, negative emotions get in the way of L2 acquisition. For L2 acquisition to happen, the *affective filter* (i.e., the inhibiting effect of negative emotions) needs to be removed.

The Natural Approach is an attempt to establish optimal and sufficient conditions for L2 acquisition. Krashen's model of language acquisition is purely theoretical and so far remains untested.

You have read about several approaches to teaching L2—all of which have some strengths and weaknesses. But which one is most effective? Educators continue to grapple with this question. Some points, however, can be made with certainty. No one language-teaching method or approach is universally applicable. Different economic and social conditions result in different learner needs and classroom environments. These, in turn, call for different language teaching methods. A child learning a second language in a situation of total immersion would arguably benefit from teaching practices that would be ineffective, or not even viable, in a situation where adults are taught to read a foreign language texts by a teacher who is not fully proficient in that language. The task of learning L2 across the entire range of skills is enormous and can only be accomplished after a prolonged period of study and—ideally—L2 immersion.

Corrective Feedback and Formal Grammar Instruction

In this section of the chapter, we are going to review some studies concerned with grammar teaching. We examine two questions: Do young students benefit from *corrective feedback* or having their errors pointed out and corrected by the teacher? And further, are L2 grammar lessons useful to young learners?

Consider the following anecdote. When leaving her school building at the end of a school day, a young ESL student realized that she had left her jacket behind. The girl ran back to the classroom and immediately spotted her jacket lying right on top of the teacher's desk. "This jacket is mines!" cried the little girl excitedly. "This jacket is *mine*," said the teacher, seizing the opportunity to teach some grammar. "It is mines!" remonstrated the girl. "It is *mine*," insisted the teacher. The child's reaction was typical. Taking no heed of the correction, she focused on the meaning of the message.[18]

The little girl's teacher used a form of corrective feedback called *recasting*. Recasting is responding to learner error by restating the utterance with an error corrected. Because recasting is nonthreatening, it is popular with teachers. That said, research findings suggest that recasts have little impact on children's L2 grammatical development.[19] A study found that students saw recasts as just another way of saying the same thing, not as corrective feedback.[20]

But maybe recasts do not work because they provide corrective feedback *implicitly*. Perhaps explicitly pointing out errors would be more beneficial to young language learners? In an important study that focused on the potential effect of explicit corrective feedback, 13 ESL students were engaged in a lesson that focused on English WH questions. The teacher called students' attention to the errors in the WH questions and provided models of correct use. The study found that corrective feedback made little difference. In all 13 subjects, there was no significant increase in the students' ability to produce well-formed WH questions.

Below is that study's transcript of a sample exchange between a student and a teacher. The student is asking a question about the time a meal was prepared and the teacher is modeling the correct form:[21]

> **Student:** *When _does her cooking_?*
>
> . . . .
>
> **Teacher:** When does she cook the dinner?
> **Student:** *When _does she cooks_ the dinner?*

But what about engaging students in rigorous practice activities? Do they provide instructional gains? In one study, 82 francophone Canadian 11- and 12-year-old children were taught a rule of English grammar. A control group made of 56 children did not get any instruction. When children were tested immediately after the lesson, those who had received grammar instruction did much better. The results of the study seemed promising. And yet, when a year later the researcher administered another test, she found that children had gone back to making the same error.[22]

Corrective feedback and formal instruction may not necessarily have immediate impact in the grade-school classroom. That said, researchers believe that young children and adolescent language learners do benefit from grammar lessons. For grammar lessons to be effective, it is critical that they meet certain criteria.

First of all, the timing of a grammar lesson is important. A lesson taught too early, when a student is not "ready," will almost certainly leave the teacher and the student frustrated. Theorists recommend providing grammar instruction when students are on the brink of mastering a form.

Second, it is important that grammar be taught in a meaningful communicative context. When students perform a grammar drill or practice a structure in isolation, they are usually bored and lost. In contrast, youngsters are much more likely to benefit from a lesson that meets their communicative needs.

Last, some methodologists advocate embedding grammar lessons in writing activities. This recommendation may strike the reader as counterintuitive. Isn't writing more demanding than speaking? And yet, combining writing with grammar instruction works because writing is both less spontaneous than speaking and more amenable to modeling.

L2 Lexicon

What is known about L2 word learning? First of all, it is important to bear in mind that L2 words are seldom learned after just one exposure. Instead, second-language word learning tends to proceed incrementally. According to some estimates, learners need as many as seven exposures to a target-language item before they begin to use it in their own speech. This incremental, gradual word learning tends to follow a pattern. Thus, passive knowledge of vocabulary usually precedes active mastery. Learners first learn to recognize new words and only later begin to produce them in oral speech and in writing. Target-like mastery of vocabulary takes a while to develop. Even proficient learners do not necessarily produce target-like collocations.

SLA studies distinguish between incidental and intentional vocabulary learning. The former involves a deliberate effort to learn new words, such as when students memorize word lists and practice new words in sentences. Incidental word learning, by contrast, involves picking up words as a by-product of meaningful activity, such as participating in a hands-on project focusing on a new concept. A great number of target words are learned incidentally, as a result of multiple exposures.

But what word-learning strategy is the most effective? One study has compared the use of different word learning strategies. Some study respondents read extensively, inferring word meaning from context; some used dictionaries; and others focused on practicing words in context. Yet another group of students wrote down words together with their translations and memorized them as lists. The researchers found that students benefited from using a combination of strategies, including reading, looking up words in dictionaries, and practicing them in context. Only one word-learning strategy—memorizing word lists—proved to be of little use.[23]

Mastery of L2 vocabulary is not complete without the mastery of *idioms*, that is, multiword units whose literal meaning is different from their actual meaning. *Does it ring a bell? My heart goes out to her, We will cross that bridge when we get there,* and *I went off the deep end* are examples of idioms used abundantly by native speakers and underused by language learners.

Implications for Instruction

1. Young language learners do not begin to speak in L2 until they are developmentally ready; there is little point in encouraging them to speak during the silent period. Learners at the pre-production stage do benefit from activities that focus on compre-hension. Students can, for instance, practice directed drawing; pantomime songs, stories, and poems; and play simple guessing games. In one comprehension-based activity, adapted from a game played by Native American children, the teacher calls out words for weather conditions (e.g., *sun, wind, cloud, rain,* or *thun-derstorm*), and the children use finger play to illustrate their mean-ings. Create a similar kinesthetic, comprehension-based activity (e.g., a hopscotch game) to teach the words for shapes, colors, and numbers.

2. Given that young language learners disregard corrective feed-back, teaching them grammar can be an uphill battle. That said, even young learners can be engaged in grammar activities. Consider an activity focusing on the modal phrase *I can* _____. Using the sentence starter *My robot can* _____, students de-scribe their imaginary robot friend (e.g., *My robot can talk, My robot can drive,* etc.). This activity works even with emerging young speakers because it includes a model and the language use is tightly controlled. Most important of all, the target pattern *I can* _____ serves a communicative function. Develop a similar activity with a focus on functional morphemes such as a preposi-tion or a pronoun. What will the students write about? What type of model will they use?

3. There is evidence that L2 words are best learned when students participate in engaging activities. Such activities work because they present words in meaningful contexts and ensure repeated exposure. Consider the following example. To teach her primary-level ESL students the words *archeological dig, pyramid,* and *Aztecs,* a teacher involved students in a role-play. The students went on an imaginary "trip" to Mexico; they climbed a "pyramid" (a stairway in the school building), participated in an "archeological dig" (rummaging through shoeboxes filled with shredded paper), found teacher-made ancient Aztec artifacts, and wrote letters

see sea cough

Figure 8.1   Using imagery to teach spelling.

home about their adventures. Create a similar role-play with a
focus on the words *Ellis Island, immigrants,* and *medical exam.*

4. An effective strategy for word learning is the keyword technique.
This technique entails creating a memorable image that learners
associate with the target word.[24] In one activity, the teacher tells
her students that *see* and *sea* are spelled differently because *see* has
two eyes, while the *a* in *sea* is really a portrait of a stingray. Similarly, the teacher uses an image to help students with the spelling
of the target word *cough.* She explains that *g* represents a person
covering her mouth when coughing, and *h* stands for the actual
sound of coughing (see Figure 8.1). What image can be used to
teach the spelling of the target item *look?*

5. An effective strategy for teaching idioms is elucidating their direct
meaning by means of pictures.[25] Students draw pictures that
portray the direct meaning of an idiom and then practice using
that idiom. For instance, learners could draw a picture of a heart
"going out" toward someone and then write a short paragraph
including the idiom *My heart goes out to her.* Design a mini lesson
that focuses on a common idiom.

WORDS TO REMEMBER

target language/L2: a second or foreign language.

SLA: second-language acquisition; an area of research concerned
with how people learn L2.

silent period: the initial stage of L2 learning in children.

rejection period: a period of adverse reaction to L2.

language transfer: applying home-language skills when learning a second language.

cognates: words that have a common origin.

negative transfer: interference of home-language skills with L2
learning.

contrastive analysis: predicting areas of difficulty for learners by comparing L1 and L2 structures.

intralingual errors: errors made by all L2 learners, irrespective of their L1.

interlingual errors: L2 errors resulting from the negative transfer of L1 skills.

interlanguage: an approximation of L2 used by learners.

creative construction: learner hypotheses with regard to L2 structure.

ultimate attainment: native-like L2 proficiency.

grammaticality judgment: learner ability to determine whether an utterance is well-formed or malformed.

sensitive period: the prepubescent years believed to be optimal for L2 learning.

linguistic intuition: native speakers' judgment as to whether a given language pattern is acceptable.

fossilization: the cessation of learning in adult SLA, as seen in the stubborn persistence of specific errors.

fundamental difference hypothesis: the belief that L2 learning is different in adults and children because only children have access to the Universal Grammar (UG).

grammar-translation method: a school of L2 teaching that uses grammar and translation activities.

direct method: a school of L2 teaching that avoids translation into L1.

audiolingual method: a school of L2 teaching that uses grammar drills performed in the lab.

communicative approach: a school of L2 teaching that emphasizes the development of learners' communication skills.

communicative competence: the ability to use the language to accomplish communication goals.

Natural Approach: an SLA theory that postulates optimal conditions for L2 acquisition.

affective filter: negative emotions that get in the way of L2 acquisition.

corrective feedback: pointing out an error.

recasting: responding to an error by repeating an utterance in corrected form.

idiom: a multiword phrase whose literal meaning is different from its actual figurative meaning.

Notes

1. Lee, C. (1996, April 18). Mute in an English-only world. *New York Times,* p. A1.
2. Itoh, H., & E. Hatch (1978). Second language acquisition: A case study. In E. M.Hatch (Ed.), *Second language acquisition: A book of readings* (pp. 76–90). Rowley, MA: Newbury House.
3. In linguistics, an asterisk is used to mark an error.
4. Taylor, B. (1975). The use of overgeneralization and transfer learning strategies by elementary and intermediate students of ESL. *Language Learning, 25*(1), 73–107.
5. Ravem, R. (1978). The Norwegian child's acquisition of English syntax. In E. M. Hatch (Ed.), *Second language acquisition: A book of readings* (pp. 76–90). Rowley, MA: Newbury House.
6. Milon, J. P. (1974). The development of negation in English by a second language learner. *TESOL Quarterly, 8*(2), 137–143.
7. Richards, J. (1971). Error analysis and second language strategies. *Language Sciences, 17,* 12–22.
8. Selinker, L. (1972). Interlanguage. *International Review of Applied Linguistics, 10,* 209–241.
9. Dulay, H. C., & Burt, M. K. (1973). Should we teach children syntax? *Language Learning, 23*(2), 245–258.
10. Krashen, S. D., Long, M. A., & Scarcella, R. C. (1979). Age, rate and eventual attainment in second language acquisition. *TESOL Quarterly, 13*(4), 573–582.
11. Snow, C., & Hoefnagel-Höhle, M. (1978). The critical period for language acquisition: Evidence from second language learning. *Child Development, 49*(4), 1114–1128.
12. Krashen, S. D., Long, M. A., & Scarcella, R. C. (1979). Age, rate, and eventual attainment in second language acguisition, *TESOL Quarterly, 13*(4), 573–582.
13. Oyama, S. (1976), A sensitive period for the acquisition of a nonnative phonological system. *Journal of Psycholinguistic Research, 5*(3), 261–283.
14. Hyltenstam, K., & Abrahamsson, N. (2001), Age and second language learning: The hazards of matching practical "implications" with theoretical "facts." *TESOL Quarterly, 35*(1), 151–170.
15. Johnson, J., & Newport, E. (1989), Critical period effects in second language learning: The influence of maturational state on the acquisition of English as a second language. *Cognitive Psychology, 21,* 60–99.
16. Selinker, L. (1972). Interlanguage. *International Review of Applied Linguistics, 10,* 209–231.
17. Bley-Vroman, R. (1980). What is the logical problem of foreign language learning? In S. Gass & J. Schachter (Eds.), *Linguistic perspectives on second language acquisition* (pp. 41–68). Cambridge, UK: Cambridge University Press.
18. Fromberg, D., personal communication.

19. Lyster, R., & Ranta, L. (1997), Corrective feedback and learner uptake: Negotiation of form in communicative classrooms. *Studies in Second Language Acquisition, 19*(1), 37–61.
20. Mackey, A., Gass, S., & McDonough, K. (2000). How do learners perceive interactional feedback? *Studies in Second Language Acquisition, 22,* 471–497.
21. Adapted from Ellis, R. (1984). Can syntax be taught?: A study of the effects of formal instructions on the acquisition of WH questions by children. *Applied Linguistics, 5*(2), 138–155.
22. White, L. (1991). Adverb placement in a second language acquisition: Some effects of positive and negative evidence in the classroom. *Second Language Research, 7*(2), 133–161.
23. Gu, Y., & Johnson, R. K. (1996). Vocabulary learning strategies and language learning outcomes. *Language Learning, 46*(4), 643–679.
24. Hulstijn, J. (1997). Mnemonic methods in foreign language vocabulary learning: Theoretical considerations and pedagogical implications. In J..Coady & T. Huckin (Eds.), *Second language acquisition: A rationale for pedagogy* (pp. 203–224). New York:Cambridge University Press.
25. Boers, F., Piquer Pritz, A., Stengers, H., & Eyckmans, J. (2009). Does pictorial elucidation foster recollection of idioms? *Language Teaching Research, 13*(4), 367–382.

9

Language Variation

It's a common story: a student goes away to college and becomes the target of teasing; the other students poke fun at the newcomer's accent. Here is how one student described this experience:

> I'm going to school in Alabama right now and I was personally excited to be around a bunch of people with Southern accents because they're so cute! haha Little did I know, that I WAS THE ONE with the "accent" and I get teased regularly...oh well. It's a good conversation starter at least.[1]

This account reflects a common perception of language. People often feel that their own speech is neutral, whereas others "have an accent." The truth is that we all speak language varieties with distinct accents or pronunciations.

Sociolinguists use the word *dialect* to refer to speech varieties used by different groups of people. Dialects are not only distinct in terms of their pronunciation: their grammars and vocabularies set them apart, too. For instance, the submarine sandwich goes by different names in different U.S.

The Educator's Guide to Linguistics, pages 127–141
Copyright © 2012 by Information Age Publishing
All rights of reproduction in any form reserved.

regions. In Philadelphia, a sign in front of a deli front says, *Philly's Best Hoagies*; whereas a New England establishment has a <u>*Grinders*</u> *Menu* displayed in its window, and a New York eatery promises *"Ten-Inch* <u>*Heroes*</u>*!"*

In the past, most studies of dialects were conducted in rural speech communities because these provided particularly rich data. Today, however, research into language variation has moved to big cities, where new urban dialects have been emerging. Whereas, before, a linguist needed to do some traveling to collect language specimens, today, they often elicit data over the phone. Below are some sample questions that a dialectologist might ask of her respondents:

> What do you call a road for automobiles? (*highway, throughway, turn-pike*, other)
> What do you call a soft drink? (*pop, soda, coke*, other)

Sometimes, it is possible to tell which dialect a person speaks based on just one revealing feature called a *shibboleth*. This word comes from the Biblical story of the battle between two Semitic tribes, the Ephraimites and the Gileadites. The Gileadites defeated the Ephraimites and set up a blockade across the Jordan River to catch the fleeing Ephraimites. The sentries asked each person who wanted to cross the river to say the word *shibboleth* (meaning "ear of corn"). The Ephraimites, whose language lacked the "sh" sound, pronounced the word with an "s" and were thereby uncovered and slaughtered.

Just like biblical characters, modern language users can spot an outsider based on a shibboleth. For instance, New Yorkers recognize out-of-towners by their pronunciation of the name *Houston Street.* Newcomers to the city will often say "Hewston," whereas New Yorkers actually say "Howston."

How is a dialect different from language? There is a commonly held belief that, in contrast to languages, dialects are *mutually comprehensible* or *mutually intelligible*—meaning that speakers of different dialects are able to understand each other. And yet, this view is not based on facts. Some pairs of languages (such as Russian and Ukrainian or Norwegian and Swedish) are mutually comprehensible, yet Ukrainian is a language, not a dialect of Russian, and Swedish and Norwegian are individual languages.

In fact, the difference between a dialect and a language has to do with status. A speech variety is a language, not a dialect, if it is held in high regard and if it takes on a full range of functions, such that it can be used for administrative, educational, legal, and political purposes. Sociolinguists joke that a language is just a dialect with an army and a navy.

Sometimes dialects are called *vernaculars*. This term is used to distinguish between standardized and unstandardized language varieties. While standardized languages have been provided with rules for correct use (codified), no such guidelines exist for vernaculars that are used in informal, colloquial situations. In contrast to standard languages, which are typically studied in school, vernaculars are picked up at home or on the street. Some examples of standard languages are Castilian Spanish, Tuscan Italian, and General American English. The Calabrian dialects of southern Italy and Brooklynese in the United States are examples of vernaculars.

The limited status of a dialect is not necessarily permanent. Over time, a dialect can develop a full range of functions and come to be accorded the status of a language. This is what happened, for instance, when the Tuscan dialect became the national language of Italy. A more recent example is when Haitian Creole was made, alongside French, the national language of Haiti. The transition from a dialect to a language is accompanied by a change in people's perceptions. When a dialect evolves into a language, it is accorded greater prestige and comes to be perceived as representing a nation.

Regional and Ethnic Variation: The Example of American English

In some countries, the local regional dialects do not have much in common with one another; in others, the opposite is true. For example, whereas speakers of regional dialects from the north and south of Germany and Italy are unable to understand each other, no such difficulty is likely to arise in France or Russia, where most local dialects resemble the standard variety used in education or the media. There are historical reasons for these differing patterns of regional variation. French and Russian regional dialects have been largely leveled because of these two countries' long-standing traditions of centralized governance and uniform education. In contrast, Italian and German regional dialects have remained more intact because these countries became unified nations only fairly recently, after centuries of being fragmented into isolated states. A great wealth of regional varieties can be found in countries with ancient cultures, such as India or China.

In the United States, sociolinguists recognize three major regional variants: the Southern, the Northeastern, and the Midland dialects. These regional variants in turn include distinct local forms, such as the Texas, Boston, and Chicago dialects. Given that the United States is a relatively young nation, its regional dialects are mutually comprehensible.

Normally, the variety spoken in a country's capital is picked as its standard language. This, however, did not happen in the United States, where the standard is based on the Midwestern dialect. How did this come about? As it happens, the norms for American English pronunciation were set by a professor from Ohio, John Samuel Kenyon (1874–1959), who authored several dictionaries of American English in the 1920s and 1940s. Because Kenyon used his own speech as the model for standard American English, to this day, the language varieties used by broadcasters and actors are based on the Midwestern pronunciation.

Let's consider just two features of standard American pronunciation that distinguish it from, say, British English. One is *r-fullness*; that is, pronouncing the *r* sound after the vowel in words such as *brother* or *mother.* The other is *flap*, or pronouncing *d* rather than *t* between vowels, so that *later* becomes "lader." Both *r*-fullness and flap are featured in Midwestern speech.

Among the three major American dialects, the Southern dialect possesses particularly strong distinguishing characteristics. One salient feature of the Southern sound system is the *pen/pin vowel merger*, in which short *e* is pronounced like short *i*, so that *ten* becomes "tin," *pen* becomes "pin," and *tender* becomes "tihnduh." In effect, in the American South, *wind* and *friend* (pronounced "frihnd") are rhyming words—a phenomenon to which the state song of Arkansas, "You Run Deep in Me," is testimony:

> Magnolia blooming, Mama smiling,
> Mallards sailing on a December <u>wind</u>.
> God bless the memories I keep recalling
> Like an old familiar <u>friend</u>.

Another feature of Southern speech is its distinctive pronunciation of the long *i* sound. While in other U.S. dialects the word *I* is pronouinced "ah-eeh," speakers of the Southern dialect simply say "aah." The "eeh" part at the end of the long 'I' sound is called glide; the phenomenon of weakening this glide is called *glide deletion*. Because of glide deletion, in the South, the sentence *When I was a child, I liked pies* becomes "Whin ah was a chahld, ah lahked pahs."

Furthermore, the Southern dialect is *r-less*, which makes it quite distinct from most American *r*-full varieties. Thus, in the South, *far* is "fah," *harm* is "hahm," and *bird* is "buhd." It is because of *r*-lessness that Southerners rhyme the words *hoorah* and *star* in the old Confederate marching song, "The Bonny Blue Flag":

Hurrah! Hurrah!
For Southern rights <u>hurrah</u>!
Hurrah! for the Bonnie Blue Flag
That bears a Single <u>Star</u>.

R-lessness has a historical explanation. In the 18th century, it became fashionable in England to drop the *r* sound, so that *large* became "lahge" and *party* became "pahty." This new pronunciation fad caught on in the U.S. South (as well as in Boston and, later, New York), but not in the west of the country. As a result, while most of the United States currently features *r*-full pronunciation, the dialects of New York, Boston, and the South are *r*-less.

A salient grammatical feature of Southern dialects, *y'all*, is similar to the Northern *you guys* and serves to distinguish between one and more than one addressee. Here is how linguist Allan Metcalf explains the use of this form:

> When one Southerner asks another, "How are y'all?" it is an inquiry about the well-being not just of the person spoken to, but also of that person's family. At a store, it is proper to ask, "Do y'all have any more of these?" where *y'all* means not just the clerk but the whole company.[2]

Like any other dialect, the Southern dialect has its own idiosyncratic vocabulary. For instance, Southerners use the word *gator* for large reptiles and call leafy green vegetables *greens*.

Alongside regional variation, the United States features a range of ethnic dialects, that is, speech forms used in diverse ethnic communities. The speech of Irish, Italian, Russian, and Native Americans, among other ethnic groups, has enriched American English with many new words. Sometimes, even grammatical features have been borrowed from ethnic dialects—a particularly interesting phenomenon. Morphemes make up a conservative linguistic subset, and it is extremely rare for them to be borrowed. It is arguably evidence of the vibrancy of American English that it has absorbed foreign suffixes such as the Russian *-nik* (e.g., *beatnik*) or the Italian *-o* (e.g., *kiddo*).

One ethnic variety that has had a particularly strong influence on American English is African American Vernacular English (AAVE). Because African American artists have been hugely influential in popular music and culture, numerous words of AAVE origin (e.g., *dig*, *bad-mouth*, *high-five*, *cool*) have gained currency in American English.

Social Variation: The Example of India

In the minds of many people, the word *dialect* is associated with regional language forms. However, alongside regional variation, there also exists language varieties used by people of different social backgrounds. Just like regional dialects, these social dialects have their own distinct words, pronunciation, and grammar.

Take the example of India, whose caste dialects have fascinated generations of anthropologists and linguists. Historically, India had four castes: the priestly caste of Brahmins; the warrior and administrative caste of Kshatriyas; the merchant caste of Vaisyas; and the farmer caste of Sudras. These four castes were said to have come from the God Brahma's mouth (the Brahmins), arms (the Kshatriyas), thighs (the Vaisyas), and feet (the Sudras). Beneath these four main castes was a fifth group: the "untouchables," or Dalits. (*Dalits* means "the downtrodden" and is the self appellation of the untouchables).

Even though the Indian constitution has pronounced these divisions illegal, to this date, the caste system continues to play a role in people's lives. Often, Indians can tell which caste a person belongs to based on his name and (especially in rural areas) his occupation. Hard menial jobs such as cleaning latrines, are performed almost exclusively by Dalits. A quota system that has been created to redress employment imbalances and facilitate Dalits' access to government jobs, has been resented by some members the upper castes, who feel they are being discriminated against and denied equal employment opportunities. Caste identity is also important in people's personal lives: many still prefer to choose spouses from within their own group.

India is a diverse, multilingual society, with 14 officially recognized regional languages and dozens of local languages and dialects. The Northern states are home to Indo-European languages such as Hindi and Punjabi. Tamil, Kannada, Malayam, and other languages of the Southern states belong to the ancient family of Dravidian languages.

Dialectologists have studied caste dialects in Indian villages (where caste divisions are more entrenched) and have identified some lexical and structural distinctions between the regional variants of Brahmin, non-Brahmin, and Dalit speech. For instance, a study conducted in a village in northern India found that members of the lowest caste, such as weavers, shoemakers, and sweepers, used pronunciation patterns not found in the dialects of the upper castes. Low-caste members nasalized their vowels; that is, pronounced them by breathing through the nose. The low-caste pronunciation was perceived by the upper castes as being "uneducated," "backward," and, interestingly enough, "old-fashioned."[3] Another study found that in the southern state of Karnata, members of different castes pronounce certain words differently. Whereas the Brahmin word for milk is *hālu*, non-Brahmins drop the *h* sound and say *ālu*. An example of a lexical difference can be seen in the words used by speakers of Kanarese when referring to movies. While Brahmins use the word *sinima*, non-Brahmins say *bayskōpu*.[4]

Two crucial concepts governing behavior in India's caste society are purity and pollution. According to traditional beliefs, members of the upper castes are defiled by association with those of the lower ones. This belief resulted in complex dietary restrictions and rules for interaction. In earlier times, even the shadow cast by an untouchable was regarded as a source of pollution. Traditionally, Brahmins and other members of the upper castes could only accept food from members of slightly lower castes.

These food-related concepts of purity and pollution are reflected in dialectal differences between castes. Research on Tamil, the language spoken in the south of India, has reported that different food-related words are used in Brahmin and non-Brahmin dialects. While non-Brahmins have one word for "food" (*sooru*) and one for "to eat" (*tinnu*), Brahmins have both neutral and pejorative words for these concepts. The neutral Brahmin word for "food" is *saadō*, and the pejorative one is *sooru*; for "to eat," the neutral word is *saapdu*, and the pejorative one is *tinnu*.[5]

Social Variation: The Example of American English

But what about the United States? What are the differences between the dialects used by members of different American social groups? An important study of such social variation in the United States was conducted by sociolinguist William Labov. Labov was especially interested in finding out how members of different social classes pronounced the postvocalic *r*; that is, the *r* sound occurring after the vowel in words such as *far* and *hard*.

Labov set up his study in three New York City stores: the upper-middle-class Saks Fifth Avenue, the middle-class Macy's, and the lower-end S. Klein. The researcher approached salespeople and asked where he could find a certain item—one that he knew was found on the fourth floor. When the salesperson provided the information, the researcher pretended he had missed the answer the first time and asked for it to be repeated. This clever strategy enabled Labov to get people to say the words *fourth floor* twice, thus eliciting four utterances containing postvocalic *r*.

Labov found that employees in the upscale stores were more likely to use postvocalic *r*, whereas those in the low-priced stores used the *r*-less pronunciation. Interestingly enough, in careful speech, when they were repeating their answers, all subjects were more likely to pronounce their *r*'s.[6] This study demonstrates that, in the United States, upper-class speakers use more *r*-full forms than speakers of lower socioeconomic status—and also that speakers switch to a more prestigious pronunciation when they feel the situation calls for it.

Another pronunciation feature that is characteristic of the speech of lower-status speakers of American English is *g-dropping*. *G*-dropping happens when verb endings are clipped, resulting in pronunciation patterns such as *readin'* and *stayin'*, rather than *reading* or *staying*. Vernacular English dialects also display certain distinctive morphosyntactic features, such as the use of *double negative*, as in *I didn't do nothing*.

Interestingly, there seem to be no linguistic features that are associated exclusively with the prestigious form of American English. The standard dialect is defined as such simply because its speakers avoid certain patterns (e.g., *r*-lessness, *g*-dropping, and double negative).

Gender Variation: The Example of Japan

Another type of language variation has to do with gender. Usually, in speech communities with distinct norms of conduct for men and women, distinctions between male and female speech are likely to be equally significant.

Consider Japan, an industrial society in which male and female roles are rather rigidly circumscribed. Whereas Japanese women are expected to act in a way that is gentle, refined, and reserved, men are expected to have a more assertive communication style. Consistent with these differing expectations for conduct and interaction, the Japanese language has distinct female and male speech forms known as *danseego* ("men's language") and *joseego* ("women's language").

One area of difference between *danseego* and *joseego* is in the use of personal pronouns. The pronoun *atashi* ("I") used by young girls and women conveys softness and femininity, whereas the male *boku* ("I") conveys masculinity. (Japanese also has a gender-neutral first-person pronoun, *watashi*).

A hit commercial for noodle soup from the 1970s capitalized on the difference between these male and female pronouns. The commercial featured a girl who said, "*Watashi tsukuru hito*" ("I am the one who cooks it"). She was then joined by a boy who yelled, "*Boku taberu hito*" ("I am the one who eats it"). (Feminist groups were outraged by the sexist ad and insisted that it be discontinued.)[7]

Another feature that distinguishes female and male Japanese speech is the use of sentence-final particles (e.g., *wa, wa yo, zo, ze*). Somewhat reminiscent of English tag questions such as *isn't it?*, and imparting a distinct tenor to speech, these particles are used differently by men and women. For instance, the female particles *wa* and *no* render speech gentle and unassertive; they engender a positive feeling and emphasize that what an interlocutor is saying is very important to the speaker.[8]

Yet another feature that sets Japanese female and male speech apart is the use of *honorifics*. Honorifics are language elements used when an individual speaks to his or her superior, to an older person, or in situations that call for the use of a formal register. Thus, the question "When are you going?" can be asked with varying degrees of politeness, depending on the honorifics used. Consider the following examples and their rough English translations:

Itse iku no? (no honorific)
("When are you going?")
Itsu iki masu ka (+ honorific)
("When is it your pleasure to go?")
Itsu ik-are masu ka (++ honorific)
("Would you be so kind as to tell me at what time you will be going?")[9]

Studies of gender variation have found that Japanese women use honorifics differently from the way men do. Japanese women opt for more polite speech varieties, involving greater use of honorifics.[10]

The media play an important role in promoting the idea that Japanese women should use language "properly." A study of Japanese female speech cites the following excerpt from a modern self-help book for women:

> It is often said that young women nowadays—whether they are students or working women—cannot use honorifics well.... I sometimes hear female teachers use the same language as male teachers.... Even in a democratic society, it's natural that there are differences in ways of talking based on sex differences, because men and women have different vocal cords.... But women dare to use men's language. Are they ignorant or lazy, or are they making foolish efforts not to be dominated by men?... Not knowing honorifics is embarrassing. Parents and teachers should teach that [to children] by showing good models.[11]

That said, Japanese culture is changing, and so are its gender-specific norms of language use. Today, men and women may use each other's dialects for expressive purposes or to redefine gender roles. In certain speech communities, such as on college campuses, speakers are more prone to "push the envelope," using forms traditionally associated with the dialect of the opposite sex. For instance, one parent told a journalist that her two college-age daughters "use more neutral, less polite and even more masculine forms of speech. Instead of ending their sentences with the feminine *wa yo*, they use *da yo*" [the masculine form].[12]

Gender Variation: The Example of American English

But what about English? Does English have gender-specific varieties? Numerous studies have demonstrated one important point of difference between male and female Englishes: that men are more prone to use nonstandard vernacular forms, whereas women are more likely to stick to the standard variety.

Note, for example, the difference in the verb ending *-ing* as it is pronounced by men and by women. Studies suggest that men have greater tendency for *g*-dropping, opting for the clipped, vernacular pronunciation of this ending. Similarly, nonstandard double negative—as in *I don't know nothing about it*—is more likely to occur in male than in female speech.

Research suggests that a preference for prestigious forms in female speech and for nonprestigious ones in male speech is a highly salient feature displayed even by small children in English-speaking speech communities. For instance, a study that focused on language use among primary-school children in New England found that the prestigious *-ing* form of the verb was used more commonly by girls, whereas boys favored the clipped, vernacular *-in'* pronunciation. Thus, whereas girls said *running, coming*, or *fishing*, boys said *runnin', comin'*, or *fishin'*.[13]

Various explanations have been offered for women's tendency to opt for more standard language use. It may be that women use standard forms to redress gender imbalances and claim a higher status in society. Given that standard forms carry greater prestige, women may use them to take care of the need to be valued and respected by others.

According to another theory, women use standard varieties because they are expected to be guardians and transmitters of social norms and values. While men can get away with rebellious and unruly behavior, societies are not likely to accept any kind of rule breaking, including the use of nonstandard language, from women.

Some sociolinguists contend that men favor vernacular language because it is associated with physical strength and manual labor and hence conveys masculinity.

Linguistic Prestige and Accommodation

Vernaculars and standard languages are not perceived in the same way. Speakers often feel that the standard variety is singularly expressive, elegant, and beautiful. In contrast, the vernacular or regional dialect may be denigrated as "crude," "uneducated," or "illiterate." Speakers of vernaculars are often criticized for what is presumed to be their sloppy or careless use of language.

It is not only people from outside vernacular speech communities who pass such judgments. Users of vernaculars themselves often suffer from *linguistic insecurity*, or a negative perception of their own speech variety. For example, speakers of low-caste dialects in India or Brooklynese may feel that their dialect is inferior to the standard form.

These negative attitudes are misconceived. It is important to bear in mind that no language form is inherently inferior. Take double negative, a salient feature of many English vernaculars. Patterns such as *I didn't do nothing* or *We didn't go nowhere* are sometimes decried as being "illogical." And yet, double negative was once a feature of standard English and is still found in standard varieties of many languages. Consider another example. While *r*-lessness may be admired in British English, this very same feature may be found crude when it crops up in Brooklynese or the Southern vernacular of American English. What these examples suggest is that the high prestige of standard dialects is related to the privileged status of their speakers. Normally, a variety used by an influential group carries higher prestige.

While non-standard language patterns are frowned upon, they are still pervasive. The popular coffee shop is called *Dunkin' Donut*, not *Dunking Donuts*. A pop singer croons *We are jammin'*, not *We are jamming*. Why do speakers opt for non-standard forms? The thing is that non-standard varieties enjoy prestige of their own. While standard varieties, are seen as being superior, people tend to perceive vernaculars as being warm, genuine, or intimate. The prestige accorded to vernaculars is known as *covert* prestige; it stands in contrast to *overt prestige* enjoyed by the standard forms.

Consider research evidence of covert prestige. A study that focused on language use among college fraternity members found that, in social situations, these speakers favored *g*-dropping, saying *hangin' out* and *playin' a game*, instead of the standard *hanging out* and *playing a game*. Apparently, the men who used these forms felt that vernacular pronunciation conveyed an image of masculinity, or of an individual who was "hard-working," "rebellious," "casual," or "confrontational."[14]

Have you ever traveled to an area with a distinct regional dialect? If so, did you notice yourself imitating the speech of the locals? Such speech modification, depending on the dialect of one's interlocutor, is called *accommodation*.

Sociolinguists recognize two types of accommodation. First, there is *convergent accommodation*, in which people adjust their speech to make it more like that of others. Convergent accommodation happens when visitors to an area interact with users of regional dialects, when adults speak to young children, or when native speakers converse with language learners. Even young children accommodate their speech. A study reported that children used more adult pronunciation patterns—at least at the beginning of the interviews. When the children felt more comfortable, they started to sound more like themselves.[15] Another study has found that college students adjusted their speech when leaving phone messages on their professors' answering machines.[16]

Generally speaking, convergent accommodation is a positive phenomenon. However, when practiced ineffectively, accommodation may result in a communication breakdown. *Overaccommodation* happens when a speaker uses excessive accommodation strategies, such as when talking to a child, an elderly person, or a person from a different educational background. When overaccommodating, the speaker may use an overly loud speech volume, a slow rate of speech, or a simplistic vocabulary, all of which may strike her interlocutor as patronizing and condescending. Because accommodation is often used unconsciously, it is important to pay attention to its potentially negative effect.

Speech adjustment may also proceed in the opposite direction, *away* from the dialect used by an interlocutor. This phenomenon is known as *divergent accommodation*. Divergent accommodation takes place when people wish to distance themselves from their interlocutors or to underscore their distinctness. For instance, a study has found that, in cross-gender conversations, men and women used more gendered speech patterns, with men employing more masculine forms and women adopting more feminine ones.[17] Another study of divergent accommodation reports that Jamaican immigrants to the United Kingdom deliberately use Jamaican Creole to sound distinct and to distance themselves from speakers of British English.[18] Similarly, a U.S. study has found that speakers of the Southern vernacular exaggerate *Y'all* and use it at every possible opportunity when interacting with those outside their community.[19]

One might think, in this age of global communication, when people are constantly exposed to standard varieties through the media, that regional and social-class-based dialects would be gravely endangered. And indeed, there is some tendency today toward the leveling-out of linguistic variation. But at least some of the more salient features of nonstandard dialects are surviving. Both the covert prestige of vernaculars and our need to accommodate to the speech of others mean that regional and social-group vernaculars are far from disappearing.

Implications for Instruction

1. ELLs often complain that, while they are able to comprehend the standard variety of the target language, they have a hard time following vernaculars or regional dialects. Discuss the extent to which linguistic variation needs to be addressed in the language classroom. Design a mini-activity that would expose language learners to a local or ethnic form of the target language.

2. It is probable that your students will be exposed to vernaculars and will pick up some nonstandard phonological or morpho-syntactic speech patterns. For instance, English language learners may pick up *g*-dropping or double negative. How are you going to handle these features in your students' speech?

3. When talking to language learners, people may use a number of accommodation strategies, including a high-volume, slow pace of speech; avoidance of idiomatic expressions; and simplified vocabulary. Discuss whether all of these strategies are effective.

WORDS TO REMEMBER

dialect: a language variant used by a local community or social group characterized by a distinct lexicon, pronunciation, and grammar.

shibboleth: a distinguishing feature of a dialect.

mutual intelligibility: a relationship between two language forms whose speakers are able to understand each other.

standard language: a language variety for which rules of proper use have been established and which takes on a full range of speech functions.

vernacular: a nonstandardized language variety learned at home and used in informal situations.

r-full/r-less pronunciation: pronouncing or leaving out the *r* sound.

flap: a feature of American English whereby a voiceless *t* is pronounced as a *d* between vowels.

pen/pin vowel merger: a pronunciation pattern in the Southern dialect of American English.

glide deletion: weak pronunciation of the terminal element in diphthongs.

g-dropping: clipped pronunciation of the *-ing* suffix.

double negative: the use of two negative forms in one phrase, as in *I didn't do nothing.*

honorifics: language forms that signal status.

linguistic insecurity: the perception that one's own language variety is inadequate.

overt prestige: a high status enjoyed by standard languages.

covert prestige: a positive attitude toward vernaculars.

accommodation: adjusting one's speech, depending on the speech of one's interlocutor.

convergent accommodation: adjusting one's speech to make it similar to the speech of one's interlocutor.

divergent accommodation: adjusting one's speech to make it different from the speech of one's interlocutor.

overaccommodation: excessive use of accommodation strategies.

Notes

1. Jodi (2011, September 29). Retrieved from http://gles.facebook.com/topic.php?uid=5589291661&topic=3661&perpage=30&start=0.
2. Metcalf, A. A. (2000). *How we talk: American regional English today.* Boston: Houghton Mifflin, p. 15.
3. Gumperz, J. (1958). Dialect difference and social stratification in a northern Indian village. *American Anthropologist, 60*(4), 668–682.
4. Bright, W. (1960). Linguistic change is some Indian caste dialects. *International Journal of American Linguistics, 26*(3), 19–26.
5. Ramanujan, A. K. (1965). *The structure of variation: A study in caste dialects.* Proceedings of the Conference on the Social Structure and Social Change in India. Chicago: University of Chicago. Cited in Bright, W. (1966). Language, social stratification, and cognitive orientation. *Sociological Inquiry, 36*(2), 313–318.

6. Labov, W. (2006). *The social stratification of English in New York City* (2nd ed.). New York: Cambridge University Press.
7. Yukawa, S., & Saito, M. (2004). Cultural ideologies in Japanese language and gender studies: A theoretical review. In S. Okamoto & J. Shibamoto Smith (Eds.), *Japanese language, gender, and ideology: Cultural models and real people* (pp. 23–37). New York: Oxford University Press.
8. McGloin, N. (1986). Feminine wa and no: Why do women use them? *Journal of the Association of Teachers of Japanese, 20*(1), 7–27.
9. Adapted from Ide, S., Hori, M., Kawasaki, A., Ikuta, S., & Haga, H. (1986). Sex differences and politeness in Japanese. *International Journal of the Sociology of Language 58*, 25–36.
10. Ibid., p. 27.
11. Okamoto, S. (2004). Ideology in linguistic practice and analysis, gender and politeness in Japanese revisited. In S. Okamoto & J. Shibamoto Smith (Eds.), *Japanese language, gender, and ideology: cultural models and real people* (pp. 38–56). New York: Oxford University Press.
12. Rudolph, E. (1991, September 1). *New York Times.* Cited in Okamoto, S. (1995). "Tasteless" Japanese: Less "feminine" speech among young Japanese women. In K. Hall & M. Bucholtz (Eds.), *Gender articulated: Language and the socially constructed self* (pp. 297–325). New York: Routledge.
13. Fischer, J. L. (1958). Social influence on the choice of a linguistic variant. *Word, 14,* 47–59.
14. Kiesling. S. (1998). Men's identity and sociolinguistic variation: The case of fraternity men. *Journal of Sociolinguistics, 2*(1), 68–99.
15. Fischer, J. (1958). Social influence on the choice of a language variant. *Word, 14,* 47–59.
16. Buzzanell, P., Burrell, N., Stafford, R., & Berkowitz, S. (1996). When I call you up and you're not there: Application of communication accommodation theory to telephone answering machine messages. *Western Journal of Communication, 60,* 310–336.
17. Hogg, M. (1985). Masculine and feminine speech in dyads and groups: A study of speech style and gender salience. *Journal of Language and Social Psychology, 4,* 99–112.
18. Edwards, V. (1985). Expressing alienation: Creole in the classroom. In N. Wolfson & J. Manes (Eds.), *Language of inequality* (pp. 325–334). Berlin: Mouton.
19. Richardson, G. (1984). Can you'all function as a singular pronoun in Southern dialect? *American Speech, 59*(1), 51–59.

10

Language Planning

Speaking comes to us as naturally as breathing. As a result, we seldom stop to think that the ways in which we learn and use languages are deeply rooted in the histories and policies of individual countries. Is your home language venerated as the symbol of a nation? What is the language's status in society? In what language were you schooled? The answers to these and a host of other questions have to do with language planning.

The term *language planning* refers to deliberate decisions societies make about language form and language use. Some countries have special agencies in charge of language planning. Old and venerable institutions such as the *Académie Française* in France, the *Real Academia Española* in Spain, and the *Accademia della Crusca* in Italy—as well as more recently created language academies in Egypt and Japan—all articulate language policies in different parts of the world. Organizations such as ministries of culture and education, publishing houses and media agencies, boards of education, and the Peace Corps also contribute to language planning.

The Educator's Guide to Linguistics, pages 143–157
Copyright © 2012 by Information Age Publishing
All rights of reproduction in any form reserved.

Language planning results in *language policies,* or language-related mandates. In this chapter, you will read about language planning and policies in different parts of the world.

Language Reform: The Example of China

The term *language reform* refers to large-scale language planning. Often triggered by significant social changes, language reform can focus on such issues as language simplification, rendering literacy more accessible, or ridding a language of foreign borrowings. While major language reforms have taken place in a number of countries (such as Turkey and Russia, both in the 1920s), arguably the largest one ever was implemented in China.

After the Communist Revolution of 1949, the new People's Republic of China launched an enormous language standardization and unification campaign meant to bolster economic and social development.

The immensity of the task was due to the country's size and linguistic diversity. The assemblage of languages spoken in China is as vast and varied as the Chinese landscape itself. In Beijing and the surrounding windswept plateaus of northern China, people speak different forms of Mandarin. On the ocean shores of southern China, they use numerous regional dialects, such as, for instance, Cantonese spoken in the province of Guandong.

Even though these languages are not mutually intelligible, Chinese people do not see their country as multilingual. Their attitude has to do with the written system of characters shared by the Chinese tongues. Words in different languages are encoded in the same characters, and people who cannot understand the oral form of a particular language are nonetheless able to glean meaning from its written text. As sinologist Robert Ramsey has put it, "When most Chinese think of a language that unites them as a people, the 'common language' they have in mind is [...] their written language."[1] It is also important to bear in mind that, throughout Chinese history, Chinese cultural minorities have been assimilated into the culture of the majority group, the Han people. This shared culture reinforces the perception of various regional languages as dialects of the same language.

The major task facing China's language reformers was establishing a common language. The colloquial (rather than formal) Mandarin spoken in Beijing, dubbed *putonghua,* or the "common language," was chosen for use in all public domains, including education, politics, and the media.

The Chinese reforms also focused on simplifying the language's written characters, some 2000 of which are now written with fewer strokes. While these simplified characters have long been popular in informal handwriting, they used to be considered "vulgar." The language reform legitimized the use of simplified characters in print. Interestingly enough, though, classical characters have not altogether disappeared. Footnotes in scholarly publications, for example, or deluxe editions of Mao Zedong's writings still use the traditional writing system.[2]

While the expansion of *putonghua* did not entail any significant changes in the Mandarin-speaking North, in other parts of the country patterns of language use have changed dramatically. When children in southern provinces start school, their teachers initially speak to them in the local dialects. However, as the school year progresses, teachers gradually switch to *putonghua* and teach children to read and write in that language. There is no formal instruction in oral *putonghua*. Since this language is seen as a dialect of Chinese, children are expected to "pick it up," which most of them do. Today, in urban centers such as Shanghai, students are proficient in both the local language and *putonghua*. In rural or economically underdeveloped areas such as Tibet, where school facilities are poor and teachers' command of *putonghua* is imperfect, children may acquire only very limited literacy skills or remain illiterate.[3] Whatever his or her level of active proficiency in *putonghua*, everybody in the country has some passive exposure to the language through ubiquitous loudspeakers, newspapers, and radio broadcasting.

Alongside characters, China uses *pīnyīn*, romanization (phonetic writing in the Latin alphabet) for teaching pronunciation and keyboard typing. One of the goals of language reform was rendering romanization more consistent. This initiative has caught the attention of Chinese computer programmers, many of whom feel that characters should be abandoned altogether on the grounds that total romanization is crucial for the development of digital technology. For now, however, the government is unlikely to embrace such radical writing reform, which would sever ties with earlier Chinese culture.[4]

What is the language situation in other Chinese-speaking areas of the world? In Taiwan, which has large numbers of ethnic Chinese whose ancestors fled the mainland after the revolution, the predominant language is Mandarin. Taiwanese print and other media use traditional (nonsimplified) characters, and the island's government has positioned itself as the champion of the classical writing system.[5] In Hong Kong, the two official languages are Cantonese and English. Since 1997, when Hong Kong transferred its sovereignty from Britain to the People's Republic of China, *putonghua* has been heard more often on the island. Tourists, shoppers, and businessmen from the mainland speak Mandarin, and the government has been promoting "trilingualism"; that is, proficiency in English, Cantonese, and *putonghua.*[6]

Linguistic Purism: The Example of France

The term *linguistic purism* refers to the belief that a language should be cleansed of foreign words, which are seen as contaminating. A paradigmatic example of a country with a purist language policy is France. Attempts to regulate language use go far back in French history. In the 17th century, Cardinal Richelieu, then chief minister to King Louis XIII, created the *Académie Française* (the French Academy), which he charged with the task of regulating French vocabulary and grammar. In the 18th century, when the quest for liberty, equality, and fraternity culminated in the French Revolution, one of the first concerns of the new government was language. In its zeal to spread republican ideas and centralize political power, the Jacobin government tried to replace the local dialects spoken by peasants with Parisian French, which was supposed to become the common language of all French citizens. As it turned out, this ambitious goal was not attainable in 18th-century France. In the 1880s, however, due to the creation of a highly centralized education system, efforts aimed at linguistic uniformity prevailed. This resulted in the disappearance of most regional French dialects.

In recent times, purist language policies in France have addressed the perceived threat of "Franglais," or the encroachment of English words upon French. In 1994, the French government passed the Toubon Act (*la loi Toubon*) meant to inhibit English borrowings. Terminology commissions have been created to coin French counterparts for English words. For example, "Walkman" was replaced by *balladeur,* "email" by *courier électronique,* and "pie chart" by *camembert.* The government advised French public servants that their "zeal for French" would be taken into account in their annual evaluations.[7] Special provisions of the Act pertain to education and the media. For instance, even when business courses in elite educational institutions are taught in English, the Act mandates that the exams be administered in French. The law also regulates the proportion of songs with lyrics in languages other than French that may be broadcasted on national radio and television.[8] Members of the French elite are particularly supportive of the Act, which they see as a shield against the spread of American commercial mass culture.

While purist attitudes typical of France have rarely been strong among English speakers, a number of other countries, such as Germany, Russia, Iceland, and Japan, have waged their own campaigns aimed at purging foreign words from their national languages. These policies, however, have seldom had long-lasting effects.

Diglossia: The Example of the Arab World

Derived from Greek, the term *diglossia* means "bilingualism"; it refers to a situation in which a speech community has two languages, with each being used for a distinct purpose. The more prestigious, high-status language (H-variety) is the language of politics, official TV and radio broadcasting, religion, and schooling. The lower-status language (L-variety) is the medium of informal interaction, popular art, and media. Diglossic speech communities often accord prestige to the H-variety, seeing it as being more grammatically correct and lexically pure. In contrast, the low-prestige L-variety tends to be viewed as primitive and ungrammatical.

While forms of diglossia exist in Haiti, southern China, and other countries, its primary example is found in the Arab world. The H-variety of the region is Classical Arabic, or *al fusha* (pronounced "ahl foos-huh"). According to Islamic belief, *al fusha* is the language in which Allah dictated the Qur'an to the Prophet Mohammed during the revelation, which began in the month of Ramadan. Revered as an inimitably beautiful, sacred language, Classical Arabic is the official language of all Arab countries.

In informal situations, however, on the street or at home, Arabs converse in local vernaculars. These include Gulf Arabic, Iraqi Arabic, Moroccan Arabic, and others. While many of these languages are mutually incomprehensible, educated Arabs are able to communicate with each other in *al fusha*, the common language of the Arab world.

Niloofar Haeri, an anthropologist from Johns Hopkins University, has traveled to Egypt to study diglossia in that country. She was particularly interested in the role of the H- and L-varieties in the lives of ordinary men and women, not only clerics or the highly educated elite. Haeri has reported that, Egyptians do not learn Classical Arabic as their mother tongue. People may first hear the language when a prayer reciter comes to their home or when they learn to pray from a parent. Formal *al fusha* lessons begin during primary school as part of religious instruction, when children memorize the five obligatory daily prayers in that language, as well as the names for the necessary ablution rituals and body positions of prostration or kneeling. In secondary school, all instruction switches abruptly to Classical Arabic. Students tend to have difficulty doing schoolwork in a language they do not speak at home. A number of Haeri's respondents remembered being berated by teachers or getting lower grades when they slipped into Egyptian Arabic.

In adult life, people experience Classical Arabic in mosques, when they hear calls to prayer, when they listen to prayer recordings in the privacy of their homes, or when they watch political programs on television. Journalists, scientists, and other individuals who have an advanced level of proficiency in *al fusha* use the language for professional interaction and writing.

There are interesting cases of code switching from the L- to H-variety. For instance, even though a politician may make a speech in local Arabic, the newspaper version of that speech will appear in *al fusha*. A young woman will read romantic verses in *al fusha* and then talk to her boyfriend using a regional vernacular.

Haeri reports that her subjects have mixed feelings about *al fusha*. While they tend to find Qur'anic texts "beautiful" (*gamiil*) and "powerful" (*quawi*) and say that the sacred language "moves them and makes them forget their daily problems," they also often have negative memories of learning it in school. Even college-educated people say that they have anxieties about making mistakes in *al fusha*.[9] Attitudes to the L-variety are also fraught with ambivalence. Egyptians find Egyptian Arabic to be lively, intimate, and humorous, but they also believe that it is grammatically sloppy and too prone to change.

Some reform-minded Middle Eastern policymakers and educators have called for language reform and the use of vernaculars as the language of instruction. Traditionalists have insisted that the current language policy remain intact. They point out that *al fusha* is a means of staying in touch with the rich Islamic culture and serves as a unifying force of pan-Arabism.[10]

Language Shift and Language Maintenance: The Example of Mexico

Some speech communities experience *language shift*, or the replacement of a less prestigious language with a more prestigious one. Language shift may happen for a variety of economic, demographic, or social reasons. Often, because proficiency in the majority language brings economic benefits, parents feel obliged to speak that language with their children. When people use a minority language in fewer situations, its stylistic registers begin to atrophy. Before long, minority-language vocabulary shrinks, and groups of words associated with various themes disappear. Language shift is also accompanied by a dramatic influx of loan words. While some borrowing is essential for normal language development, in cases of language shift, the use of loan words from a dominant language may result in the catastrophic erosion of the minority-language vocabulary. As language shift progresses, speakers lose their ability to create new sentences in the minority language and become able to produce only a limited number of formulaic utterances. In extreme cases, the minority language comes to be used only in religious rituals or for ceremonial purposes.

An example of a language affected by language shift is Nahuatl (pronounced "nah wahtl), once the language of the formidable Aztec empire and now a minority language in Mexico. (Although you may not be aware of it, you already know some words of Nahuatl origin: *avocado, coyote,* and *tomato* are derived from the Nahuatl *ahuacatl, coyotl,* and *tomatl* and entered English via Spanish.)

The bloody conquest of the Aztec Empire by the Spanish conquistadors, with their policies of enslavement and genocide, gradually pushed the Aztec languages to the fringes of Mexican society. Today, Nahuatl mostly survives in remote rural communities. Members of these communities are referred to as *indios* or *indigenas,* and their language is commonly called *Mexicano.* Ethnically, speakers of Nahuatl are not markedly different from other Mexicans, the vast majority of whom are either of mixed Native American and European or pure Native American lineage. It is their use of Nahuatl and adherence to Indian traditions, beliefs, and dress that distinguish so-called *indios* from other Mexicans.[11]

While Spanish enjoys a high status in Mexico and is associated with "speaking Christian," Nahuatl has no prestige and is denigrated by its speakers themselves as backward. One study describes Nahuatl speakers who, even though they knew who the Aztecs were, did not realize "that the language they spoke was a modern variety of the language of the Aztecs."[12] This study also provides evidence that some Nahuatl speakers avoid using the language within earshot of monolingual Spanish speakers, so as not to call attention to their *indio* status. One village dweller told the researcher that "when he goes to a store in the city [...] with a friend or family member who speaks only Nahuatl, they strategize in advance about how to conduct transactions without resorting to communication in Nahuatl." Typically, the Nahuatl monolingual will remain silent while his or her bilingual companion makes inquiries of the salesperson in Spanish.[13]

In 2008, in an effort to reverse the process of Nahuatl decline, the Mexican government mandated that the language be taught in schools. There are also plans to offer courses in Nahuatl at universities. Similar *language maintenance* programs meant to reverse language shift are currently underway in many countries. For example, Guatemala has established a Commission for the Official Recognition of Indigenous Languages; Nicaragua has authorized some teaching in the Miskito language, and Peru has established academies for Quechua.[14] As encouraging as these developments are, however, such programs cannot be truly successful unless the larger society confers prestige on a minority language—and unless speakers of a minority language are proud of their linguistic and cultural heritage.

Language Death: The Example of Australia

Language death, or language disappearance, happens when a language no longer has any native speakers. Languages can die overnight, such as when a language community is wiped out by a natural disaster or genocide, or they can die gradually as the result of language shift. If speakers of a minority language give up teaching the language to their children, only elderly speakers of the language will be left in the speech community. Once the language has only a few dozen elderly speakers, it is considered moribund, or gravely endangered. The moment its last speaker dies, the language is dead.

Hundreds of languages have died in the course of human history. Some, such as Latin and Ancient Greek, have left us written records, but most have disappeared without a trace. In the 21st century, due to mass migration, industrialization, and resulting language shifts, languages are dying at an unprecedented rate. By conservative estimates, half of the world's 6,000 languages will disappear during this century.

Language death entails a loss for all humanity. When a language ceases to exist, with it disappears a unique culture-specific worldview, a trove of folk knowledge, and invaluable information about the history and culture of a people.

Consider the case of aboriginal Australian languages. Once dismissed by colonizers as "primitive," these languages are now the object of scientific scrutiny. Scientists are fascinated by their grammatical complexity and conceptual richness. To take just two examples, the Oenpelli python has the long-established name *nawaran* in one of the aboriginal languages, but was not identified as a distinct species by Western scientists until the 1960s. Similarly, quite recently, due to the availability of digital imaging, Western scientists have realized that the best way to classify wallabies, kangaroos, and other macropods is based on their manner of hopping. Yet aboriginal languages have long had different verbs to distinguish between the hopping of macropod males and females, as well as between young and adult animals.[15]

Tragically, most of the roughly 500 Australian languages that existed before contact with Europeans have disappeared. Smallpox epidemics triggered by colonization, the crowding of Aborigines into missions, and the poisoning of waterholes led to widespread loss of life and concomitant language death. Today, there are 24–25 fully functional aboriginal languages in Australia and about 120 more in various stages of endangerment.[16]

In recent years, there has emerged a growing public awareness of the plight of endangered languages. Various organizations are now working to preserve languages that are moribund. Scientists go to the Siberian taiga, the Amazon jungle, and the Australian bush to interview surviving elderly speakers and create audio and written records of languages at the brink of extinction.

There have also been some attempts at *language revival*, or the restoration of a dead language. However, with the notable exception of the revival of Hebrew, Israel's official language, language revival programs have had mixed success. Teaching adults a dead heritage language is hard, both logistically and cognitively.

Language Rights: The Example of the Kurdish Language

Language rights are the rights of individuals and communities to choose a language for private and public use in certain areas, such as education, media, law, and art.

In some countries, repressive policies prevent minority groups from exercising their language rights. Take the example of the Kurds, members of a minority group of approximately 30 million people who inhabit the oil-rich mountain regions of Iran, Iraq, Turkey, and Syria. For generations, Kurds have been struggling—sometimes violently—to maintain their cultural identity and to gain some measure of political autonomy. Wary about Kurdish separatism, the governments of Iran, Iraq, Turkey, and Syria have suppressed Kurdish nationalist movements. To prevent Kurds from rallying around their language, the four countries' authoritarian regimes have enforced assimilative policies that have curtailed or banned the use of Kurdish.

In Turkey, Kurds compose an estimated 20% of the population. The Kurds are ethnically and culturally distinct from the majority Turkish population. The Turkish authorities, however, have denied this distinctness, claiming that the Kurds only developed a separate culture because they live in an isolated mountainous area. The Turkish government infamously referred to the Kurds as "mountain Turks" and banned the use of the Kurdish language. Article 26 of the 1982 Turkish constitution stated: "No language prohibited by law shall be used in the expression and dissemination of thought. Any written or printed documents, phonograph records, magnetic or video tapes, and other media instruments used in contravention of this position shall be confiscated."[17] At one point, in order to obliterate all traces of Kurdish culture, the Turkish authorities initiated a campaign to replace Kurdish place names with Turkish ones.

To date, the ban on the use of Kurdish has been lifted in Turkey. In August 2002, the Turkish Parliament, then applying for membership in the European Community, passed laws abolishing the death penalty and permitting the use of Kurdish in broadcasting and education.[18] In 2009, the government presented a landmark plan calling for the free use of the Kurdish language and restoring Kurdish names to towns. However, the country's only pro-Kurdish party in parliament has been disbanded.[19]

In Syria and Iran, where Kurds constitute 10% and 7% of the population, respectively, the governments have been enforcing policies aimed at assimilating the Kurdish minority. In Syria, these measures have included a ban on the use of Kurdish, the replacement of Kurdish place names with Arabic ones, and bans on schooling and publication in Kurdish.[20] The Iranian government has also repressed Kurds. According to a Kurdish Iranian writer, her mother, "fearing prison and [the] torture of her children," had been forced four times in her life to burn "the few Kurdish books and records we [the family] had acquired clandestinely."[21]

In Iraq, where Kurds account for some 20% of the population, the repression of the Kurdish language has been particularly harsh. The Kurdish language was banned in Iraqi media and education. After the Kurds sided with Iran during the Iran-Iraq War of 1980–1988, the response of Iraqi dictator Saddam Hussein was brutal. Hussein razed Kurdish villages and killed thousands of civilians with chemical weapons.

The toppling of Saddam Hussein's regime presented Iraqi Kurds with unique opportunities. The new Iraqi constitution grants Kurdish the status of the country's second official language. The constitution does not, however, grant the Kurds a right to secede.[22]

There is an emerging awareness in the modern world that language rights are an important subset of human rights. International covenants, charters, and international organizations promote public and individual language rights. For example, in 1996, the Organization for Security and Cooperation in Europe issued documents concerning language-rights violations suffered by the Roma people or Gypsies.[23] In 2005, the East-West Center in Washington, D.C., put forth a set of recommendations for the development of language policies pertaining to the Uyghurs, the 10-million-strong Muslim minority residing in the northwestern border region of China.[24]

Official Language: The Example of American English

An official language is a language that has special legal status in a country. Usually, the official language is used in official contexts, such as the government, courts, education system, and public media.

A dialect can become the official language of a country if it is held in high esteem by the people. For instance, what we now call standard Italian—the Florentine version of the Tuscan dialect—became the official language of Italy because it was the language of many revered artists and writers of the Italian renaissance.

Picking an official language may stir great controversy. For instance, after colonial India won its fight for independence, Mahatma Gandhi and his followers wanted to make Hindi the new state's official language. However, in multilingual India, those people who did not speak Hindi met the plan with great resistance. Eventually, a compromise was reached. Not only English, which was spoken by many educated people, but also several other languages, including Hindi, Punjabi, and Bengali, were all given the status of India's so-called "scheduled" or official languages.

In contrast to the situation in many other countries that have official languages, no special legal status is granted to U.S. English. As revealed by a 1987 survey, many Americans are unaware of this fact and presume that English is the country's official language.

Scholars disagree as to why English is not enshrined in the U.S. Constitution. Some say that the founding fathers disagreed in principle with infringing upon the language liberties of the new nation's citizens. As writer James Crawford puts it, "This country has a kind of libertarian tradition where language is concerned—a democracy is not supposed to tell its citizens how to talk—which may explain the Founders' 'oversight' when it came to mandating an official tongue."[25] Other scholars point out that English was not made the official language because it already enjoyed de facto dominant status. When the dominant role of English was placed in jeopardy by the purchase of French-speaking Louisiana, Benjamin Franklin insisted that more English-speaking colonists settle the new territory.

The controversy surrounding the official status of English became particularly heated during the 1980s. In 1981, California Senator Samuel Hayakawa, a Canadian immigrant of Japanese ancestry, proposed a bill to make English the official language of the United States. "English has long been the main unifying force of the American people," contended Hayakawa. "But now prolonged bilingual education in public schools and multilingual ballots threaten to divide us along language lines."[26] Although the bill died in the lower house, Hayakawa was not discouraged. In 1983, he put together a Washington lobby group called "U.S. English" and spearheaded what came to be known as the *English Only* movement, a multimillion-dollar campaign to make English the official language of the United States. Among the movement's supporters were renowned public figures, such as writers Saul Bellow and Gore Vidal and journalist Walter Cronkite, as well as countless ordinary citizens who embraced the cause.

The English Only movement met with harsh criticism from the Hispanic community, whose members felt that English Only had an anti-Hispanic bias and was motivated by the Anglo community's sense of demographic insecurity. "U.S. English is to Hispanics as the Ku Klux Klan is to blacks," charged Raul Yzaguirre, president of the National Council of La Raza.[27]

In 1988, the *Arizona Republic* published a document that suggested there was some basis for the mistrust attached to the English Only movement. The document leaked to the press was a memorandum written by John Tanton, a Michigan ophthalmologist and cofounder of U.S. English. In a note intended for internal use, Tanton warned that, due to the high birthrate of Hispanic families, Hispanic Americans would outnumber Anglo children and eventually take over the country:

> Gobernar es poblar translates "to govern is to populate." In this society where the majority rules, does this hold? Will the present majority peaceably hand over its political power to a group that is simply more fertile? Can homo contraceptivus compete with homo progenitiva [*sic*] if borders aren't controlled? Perhaps this is the first instance in which those with their pants up are going to get caught by those with their pants down! As Whites see their power and control over their lives declining, will they simply go quietly into the night?[28]

The ensuing scandal caused Tanton to resign from U.S. English. Some of the movement's high-profile supporters also dissociated themselves from the organization.

The debate around the status of English in the United States is ongoing. Proponents of English Only argue that English is the glue that holds the fabric of the nation together and that the weakened status of English will result in the fragmentation of society. They also claim that, unlike previous generations of newcomers, contemporary immigrants are unpatriotic, come to the United States with the intention of returning to their home countries, and often fail to learn English.

To counter these alleged social ills, the English Only movement advocates various types of policy changes. Some members demand that English be given emblematic status and recognized as a symbol of the United States. Others propose that English be made the only language used in the political domain, and that election materials such as ballots only be printed in English. Still others demand that an English-language proficiency test be required for immigrants who apply for U.S. business licenses. In the educational sphere, demands range from a ban on bilingual education to suggestions that school documentation, such as notices and letters to parents, only appear in English.

Opponents of the English Only movement point out that the United States residents are brought together by their commitment to liberal and democratic ideas, not the traditional attributes of a nation, such as religion, race, or language. They argue that the English Only legislation is divisive and mean-spirited. They also contend that immigrants are more likely to become loyal U.S. citizens, if they are given access to quality education, effective English language instruction and—as a consequence—access to upward mobility.

Still, the English Only movement is going strong. To date, in response to the English Only movement, more than 30 states have adopted laws that make English their official language. In most cases, the official status of English is symbolic.

Implications for Instruction

1. Language policies in sending countries have tremendous implications for ESL instruction. The quality of language teaching in the home country, the language of schooling, and societal attitudes to language all impinge on the child's experience of learning ESL. Conduct a project investigating language policies in a sending country (e.g., Cuba, El Salvador, Haiti, or Korea). Research those language policies that pertain to education.
2. Language shift is pervasive in immigrant communities. This is unfortunate and even tragic because the loss of a home language means severing a vital link to the language learner's family and culture. Conduct a study of language shift in an immigrant community. Study language attitudes and patterns of language use. Discuss strategies for encouraging students to maintain their home languages.
3. Research the history and current status of the proposal to make English the official language of the United States. How might change in the status of English affect English language learners?

WORDS TO REMEMBER

language planning: decisions societies make about language form and language use.

language policies: language-related mandates.

language reform: large-scale language planning that often involves language simplification and renders literacy instruction more accessible.

language rights: the rights of individuals and communities to choose a language for use in private and public spheres.

official language: a language that has special legal status in a country and is used in all official domains.

English Only: the movement to establish English as the official language of the United States.

purism: the belief that foreign words contaminate language purity.

diglossia: a situation where a speech community uses two languages, with each one having a distinct purpose.

language shift: the replacement of a minority language by a majority language.

language maintenance: efforts aimed at reversing language shift.

language death: language disappearance that happens when the last speaker of a language dies.

language revival: the restoration of a dead language.

Notes

1. Ramsey, R. (1987). *The languages of China*. Princeton, NJ: Princeton University Press, p. 17.
2. Ibid.
3. Dreyer, J. T. (2003). The evolution of language policies in China. In M. Brown & S. Ganguly (Eds.), *Fighting words: Language policy and ethnic relations in Asia* (pp. 353–384). Cambridge, MA: MIT Press.
4. Ramsey, R. (1987). *The languages of China*. Princeton, NJ: Princeton University Press.
5. Ibid.
6. Zhang, B., & Yang, R. (2004). *Putonghua* education and language policy in postcolonial Hong Kong. In M. Zhou & H. Sun (Eds.), *Language policy in the People's Republic of China: Theory and practice since 1949* (pp. 143–162). Boston: Kluwer Academic.

7. Spolsky, B. (2004). *Language policy.* Cambridge, UK: Cambridge University Press, P. 67.
8. Wright, S. (2004). *Language policy and language planning: From nationalism to globalization.* New York: Palgrave Macmillan.
9. Haeri, N. (2003). *Sacred language, ordinary people.* New York: Palgrave Macmillan, p. 39.
10. M. Maamouri. (1998, September). *Language education and human development: Arab diglossia and its impact on the quality of education in the Arab region. Proceedings of Mediterranean Development Forum* (Marrakech, Morocco), International Literacy Institute, University of Pennsylvania. Retrieved January 17, 2006, from http://www.worldbank.org/wbi/mdf/mdf2/papers/humandev/education/maamouri.pdf.
11. Riding, A. (1984). *Distant neighbors: A portrait of the Mexicans.* New York: Knopf.
12. Ibid., p. 11.
13. Ibid., p. 10.
14. Spolsky, B. (2004). *Language policy.* New York: Cambridge University Press.
15. Evans, N. (1998). Aborigines speak a primitive language. In L. Bauer & P. Trudgill (Eds.), *Language myths* (pp. 159–168). London: Penguin Books.
16. Wurm, S. (2003). The language situation and language endangerment in the Greater Pacific Area. In M. Janse & S. Tol (Eds.), *Language death and language maintenance: Theoretical, practical and descriptive approaches* (pp. 15–47). Amsterdam: John Benjamins.
17. Gunter, M. (1988). The Kurdish problem in Turkey *Middle East Journal, 42*(3), 389–406.
18. Spolsky, B. (2004). *Language policy.* New York: Cambridge University Press.
19. Dagher, S. (2011, October 20). Kurds. *New York Times.* Retrieved from http://topics.nytimes.com.
20. Spolsky, B. (2004). *Language policy.* New York: Cambridge University Press.
21. Hassanpour, A. (2000). The politics of a-political linguistics: Linguists and linguicide. In R. Phillipson (Ed.), *Rights to language equity, power, and education: Celebrating the 60th birthday of Tove Skutnabb-Kangas.* Mahwah, NJ: Erlbaum, p. 36.
22. Bakery, H., & Laipson, E. (2005). Iraqi Kurds and Iraq's future. *Middle East Policy, 12*(4), 66–76.
23. Spolsky, B. (2004). *Language policy.* New York: Cambridge University Press.
24. Dwyer, A. M. (2005). The Xinjing conflict: Uyghur identity, language policy and political discourse. *Policy Studies No. 15.* Washington, DC: East-West Center.
25. Crawford, J. (1992). *Hold your tongue: Bilingualism and the politics of "English Only."* Reading, MA: Addison-Wesley, p. x.
26. Ibid., p. 4.
27. Ibid., p. 148.
28. Ibid., p. 151.

11

Language Change

When we speak to much older or younger people, we cannot help notic-ing that their speech is slightly different from ours. The difference is there because language changes over time. Words, as well as speech sounds and grammar, are in a state of perpetual flux.

You may have observed some changes in the English language dur-ing your own lifetime. For instance, there has recently been a change in English intonation. Although English statements generally have a falling tone, some speakers have begun making statements with a rising intonation (e.g., *What did you do yesterday? I went shopping?*). This high-rising terminal (HRT), popularly known as "uptalk," was first observed in New Zealand, Australia, and on the U.S. Southwest coast. It has since spread to many other English-speaking communities. HRT is especially prevalent among young women. Some linguists believe that women, who tend to have a more cooperative communication style, use HRT when they seek affirmation from their interlocutors.

Another recent change is in the realm of grammar. Linguistic studies have reported that English modal verbs, such as *must* and *will*, have gradu-

The Educator's Guide to Linguistics, pages 159–175
Copyright © 2012 by Information Age Publishing
All rights of reproduction in any form reserved.

ally been falling out of use. Instead of these modal auxiliaries, speakers have been using phrases such as *have to, supposed to,* and *going to.* Thus, in a situation where 1960s speakers of English would have said, *You must do it,* modern English speakers are much more likely to say, *You have to do it.*[1]

More often than not, language change is spontaneous; innovation usually takes place for no apparent reason. In other instances, however, changes can be accounted for by speakers' need to communicate more efficiently. Take the changes in English writing brought about by email and text messaging. New forms such as *lol, lmao, fyi, omg,* and *wtf* enable writers to communicate more quickly and with less effort.

We have just discussed three language changes that have taken place in recent years. But how has English changed over the long course of its existence? What was it like originally? Can speakers stop a language from changing? These are some of the questions we tackle in this chapter.

Old English (OE): Lexicon, Pronunciation, and Grammar

To get an idea of what English was like in its initial stages, we will have to make an imaginary trip back in time to the 5th century A.D. Our destination will be the southern part of modern-day Great Britain. This is where language historians have discovered the earliest traces of the English language.

In the distant past, the British Isles were inhabited by the Celts, the ancestors of the modern Irish, Scottish, and Welsh peoples. The Celtic tribes had a fairly developed culture, with a writing system and a complex set of religious beliefs. For many years, the Celts were governed by the Romans, who had conquered the British Isles and ruled over the greater part of Europe.

The Celts coexisted relatively peacefully with the Romans and enjoyed the protection of the Roman military. But the Roman dominion over the British Isles ended abruptly after Rome was sacked by the Visigoths in A.D. 410. Almost overnight, the Western Roman Empire crumbled, and the Romans had to pull their legions out of the provinces. Suddenly, the Celts found themselves without protection against their neighbors' aggression.

At that time, three particularly warlike groups came sailing across the North Sea from the territory of today's Germany and Denmark to pillage the Celts' villages and seize their rich pastures. These were the Angles, the Saxons, and the Jutes. Over the course of approximately 100 years, the Anglo-Saxons (as these invaders are now collectively called) pushed the Celts to the periphery of the island and took over their land. The beginnings of the English language can thus be traced to the 5th century A.D., when the

Roman Empire fell and the Anglo-Saxons—having ousted the Celts—first settled on the territory of modern-day Great Britain.

In modern North American English, the words "Anglo-Saxon culture" connote wealth and privilege. The early Anglo-Saxons, however, were anything but genteel. They were members of a society made up primarily of farmers and warriors. In the 5th century, the average Anglo-Saxon lived in a windowless house with sunken floors, worked the land for food and clothing, and had a brutally short lifespan. Historians report that only 10% of Anglo-Saxon men lived past the age of 40, and that more than half the women had died by the age of 30.[1]

The Anglo-Saxons called the language they spoke *Englisc;* modern language historians refer to it as *Old English* or *Anglo-Saxon.* Only a fraction of Old English words have survived in Modern English. And yet, though relatively few in number, they make up the core of today's English vocabulary. Prepositions, articles, and also some nouns, such as *ground* (from Old English *grund*), *blood* (from *blōd*), and *sword* (from *sweord*), as well as verbs, such as *eat* (from *etan*), are among the oldest words in the language.

If you heard Anglo-Saxons speaking Englisc, you would not have been able to follow the conversation. This is because most Anglo-Saxon words have become obsolete and are no longer part of Modern English. Gone are the words *ādloma* ("one crippled by fire"), *burh* ("fortified settlement"), *feorm* ("provision of food to traveling landlords"), *þegn* ("vassal, retainer"), and countless others.

And there is yet another reason why you would have been unable to follow a conversation between Anglo-Saxons: Old English pronunciation was drastically different from that of Modern English.

To experience the sounds of Old English, consider the first line of the Christian Lord's Prayer: "Our Father, who art in heaven, hallowed be thy name." In Old English, these words were written as follows: "*Fæder ūre, þu þe eart on heofonum, si þin nama gehalgod*" (Literally: "Father our, you who are in Heavens, be your name hallowed"). Read this line out loud several times, pronouncing each word exactly the way it is spelled (in Old English, spelling and pronunciation matched). But note that the sound of the letter "æ" is like the *a* sound in c<u>a</u>t, that "þ" is interdental, like *th*, and that the first *g* in *gehalgod* is pronounced with a *y* sound. Listen to the sounds of Old English as you are reading, and see for yourself how different they were from those of Modern English.

Now that you have some idea of Old English pronunciation, let us discuss in more detail just one of its features: its long vowels. Anglo-Saxons pronounced long vowels differently from the way we pronounce them today. For instance, the word *nama* in the Lord's Prayer was pronounced "nahmah." Below is a list of some more Old English words with long vowels. Note that in all seven cases, the long vowels had *continental pronunciation*; that is, their pronunciation and spelling matched.

Old English	Translation	Pronunciation
tīma	time	"teehmah"
grēne	green	"grehneh"
brecan	break	"brehkahn"
nama	name	"nahmah"
bāt	boat	"baaht"
mōna	moon	"mohnah"
hūs	house	"hoohs"

Let us now say a few words about Old English grammar. Old English was an *inflected language*; that is, it used a rich system of bound morphemes to mark grammatical relations. If you have studied Spanish, German, or Russian, you are already familiar with how inflected languages work. Old English was similar. It used endings to show, for instance, if the verb was used in the first, second, or third person. Thus, when an Anglo-Saxon woman referred to her own possessions, she said, "*ic hæbbe*" ("I have"); if she addressed her husband, she said, "*þū hæfst*" ("you have"); and she said, "*hē hafþ*" ("he has") when she referred to her neighbor.

Another distinguishing feature of Old English was its use of *vowel mutation*, or a change in a word's stem vowel, to mark grammatical meaning. For instance, the plural form of the noun *fōt* ("foot") was *fēt* ("feet"). This pattern of marking plurality was much more common in Old English than in Modern English; for instance, the plural of *bōc* ("book") was *bēc* (pronounced "behch").

Another Old English morphological process was *ablaut*, a vowel change that marked the past tense of the so-called strong verbs. For instance, the past tense of *standan* ("stand") was *stōd* ("stood"). Like vowel mutation, this morphological process was pervasive in Old English. Old English had hundreds of strong verbs; the past tense of *helpan* ("help"), for instance, was *healp*.

As you can see, Old English was quite different from Modern English. But when and how did things change? Some major developments that took place during the Middle and Early Modern periods of English are discussed in the next section of this chapter.

Middle English (ME): Some Lexical and Grammatical Changes

Modern scholars use the name *Middle English* to refer to the English that was spoken during the Middle Ages. Linguists date the start of Middle English to 1066, perhaps the single most important year in the history of the English language. It was the year when Anglo-Saxon England was invaded by an offshoot of the Vikings, a mighty seafaring people who had long raided English villages, slaughtering peasants and looting their property. The Vikings who sailed to the English shore in 1066 were called Normans. They spoke French and came from the region of France known to this day as Normandy. The Normans were led by William, Duke of Normandy, who had a claim to the English throne.

The news of the Norman invasion reached the English King Harold after he had just finished fighting off an invasion of Norwegian Vikings in the north. All the same, he immediately led his men south to confront the new enemy. The two forces clashed near the village of Hastings. The Normans were ruthless and tactically shrewd; they feigned retreat and, when the English army broke ranks to pursue them, counterattacked with a vengeance. Then happened one of those accidents that would never occur in modern warfare: King Harold, who fought alongside his men, was killed. The leaderless English army was decimated. This bloody combat went down in history as the Battle of Hastings. In the months following this fateful battle, the Normans conquered all of England.

In the years after the Conquest, the new King William (William the Conqueror) confiscated the land of rebellious English earls and handed it over to Norman lords who erected enormous stone castles to protect their new possessions. William also replaced the Anglo-Saxon clergy with Norman priests and ordered the construction of imposing cathedrals. To this day, the medieval Norman structures dotting the English countryside convey a message of might. In post-Conquest England, Normans held all the positions of power, and French culture was the culture of prestige.

The Conquest's impact on language was enormous. England had become a bilingual society. Whereas medieval English peasants and townsfolk still spoke English, the upper classes conversed in French. It is said that King William tried to learn English but soon gave up the attempt. Anglo-Norman barons never learned to speak English either—though it is said that some used it for swearing! In post-Conquest England, English was looked down upon as the crude and uncultivated language of a socially inferior class.

At the time, it seemed as though English would never regain its position. And yet in the face of all odds, English stood its ground. There were a number of reasons for the resurgence of English. The first one was social. Because French and English nobles intermarried, French and English children played together, and the French upper classes employed English-speaking servants, the use of English by the upper classes became more common. Another reason for the replacement of French with English was demographic. The Black Death (the bubonic plague epidemic) killed off huge numbers of people in the Middle Ages, creating in its wake a shortage of labor force. In the years following the plague, English men of labor were emboldened by the demand for their skills and were no longer self-conscious about speaking English. Yet another reason behind the resurgence of English was political. The dynastic wars between England and France made a return to English a necessity: the Anglo-Norman kings needed to use English to rally their own subjects against the French enemy. As a result, 300 years after the Conquest, English had returned to widespread use.

English survived the Conquest, but it reemerged profoundly transformed. The change was particularly great in the realm of vocabulary. On the one hand, approximately 85% of Anglo-Saxon words had become obsolete. On the other hand, English now expanded tremendously, as it acquired thousands upon thousands of Latin and French loanwords. The number of French borrowings in English is huge: By some estimates, 10,000 French words became part of the English lexicon in the post-Conquest years. Most of these words were from the fields of law and administration; others had to do with medicine, art, and fashion.

In the field of administration, English adopted words such as *government, liberty, majesty, manor, mayor, parliament, peasant, prince, tax, treasurer,* and *treaty.* In the area of religion, English words of French origin include *abbey, cathedral, charity, clergy, creator, prayer, religion, virgin,* and *virtue.* French-English words from the realm of law include *accuse, arrest, felon, judge, prison, punishment,* and *warrant.* In the military sphere, there are also many French borrowings, such as *army, battle, captain, combat, defend, enemy, soldier, spy,* and *vanquish.* The words listed here are only a small fraction of the French vocabulary that has become an inalienable part of English. We use them without stopping to think of their foreign origin.

One effect of the Norman invasion is the distinctive structure of the English lexicon. While words associated with labor tend to be Anglo-Saxon, those that refer to leisure activities are French. Consider the following list of Anglo-Saxon and French words. These word pairs illustrate the mores of Anglo-Norman society. While the Anglo-Saxon peasants labored, their French-speaking overlords feasted.

Anglo-Saxon	French
cow	beef
lamb	mutton
pig	pork
deer	venison

Another source of borrowings was Latin, the spoken language of medieval clergymen and scholars. Latinate words such as *abject, custody, history, incarnate, incredible, juniper, mechanical, rosary, subjugate, subdivide, supplicate,* and scores of others were borrowed into English from theological and scholastic treatises.

This widespread borrowing from French and Latin lent a peculiar trait to the English lexicon. Many English words have duplicates of French and Latin origin. Moreover, English has a consistent pattern in its synonymy: whereas the Anglo-Saxon word is usually shorter and more common, its French equivalent is often more literary, and its Latin one scholarly. Consider the following examples:

English	French	Latin
rise	mount	ascend
ask	question	interrogate
goodness	virtue	probity
fear	terror	trepidation
holy	sacred	consecrated
time	age	era

Because the meanings of the words in these triads are close, but not identical, speakers of English are able to express the subtlest distinctions in meaning. It is said that English has one of the most extensive lexicons of all the world's languages.

Let us now listen to the voice of a medieval English poet who composed his verse in three languages—Latin, French, and English—all of which had currency in medieval England:

Scripsi hec carmina in tabulis;
mon ostel est en mi la vile de Paris;
may y sugge namore, so wel me is;
ʒef hi deʒe for loue of hire, duel hit ys.

"I have written these verses on my tablets;
my lodging is in the middle of the city of Paris;
let me say no more, I feel such joy;
if I die for love of her, it would be a pity."

Note the trilingualism of this bittersweet youthful poem. The poet uses Latin, the language of schooling, when he mentions his writing tablets; he uses French to talk about his life in Paris, where he probably moved to attend the university; and he professes his love in English, his native language.

Middle English did not only grow lexically. It was also affected by profound grammatical changes. One important development was the *falling together* or *leveling of inflections*, the process whereby various word endings came to have a similar pronunciation and eventually vanished entirely. Thus, verbal person markers (e.g., *ic hæbbe̱*, *þū hæf̱s̱ṯ*, etc.) were almost completely lost. This loss of inflections was particularly intensive in Middle English and carried through to its logical conclusion in Modern English. Today, only a few remnants of the rich Anglo-Saxon system of bound morphemes have survived. One is the ending *-s* used in the third-person singular. And the aftershocks of the Middle English leveling of inflections are not yet over. Some speakers of Modern English drop even the *-s* ending, producing forms such as *She go there.*

Additionally, in Middle English, the use of vowel mutation to form the plural of nouns (*book/bec*) and the use of ablaut to form the past tense (*help/healp*) ceased being productive. Consequently, certain forms in Modern English, such as *foot/feet* or *give/gave*, have become grammatical irregularities. In several other instances, the old and new forms are in competition (e.g., *sneak/sneaked* but also *snuck*). For the most part, though, Modern English uses the ending *-s* to mark the plural of nouns and the *-ed* ending to mark the past tense (e.g., *faxe̱s̱*, *Xerox̱eḏ*).

The reasons for the decay of inflections are unclear. It may have had something to do with the English stress pattern. You may recall from Chapter 2 that English endings are unstressed and tend to be pronounced indistinctly. The stress–unstress pattern, the hallmark of English since its early days, may have brought about the erosion of Old English inflections. Some scholars speculate that in the situation where French-speaking noblemen did not pay much attention to the lower classes' way with language, common people became more likely to drop their word endings.

While the impact of the Norman Conquest on English grammar remains somewhat unclear, it certainly did enrich the English vocabulary. It also had huge sociopolitical consequences. Norman rule unified the once-fragmented Anglo-Saxon society and helped the country resist powerful foreign invaders.

As a new, stronger nation, post-Conquest England was prepared to turn the last page of the Middle Ages and enter the age of the Renaissance.

Early Modern English (EME): Some Lexical and Pronunciation Changes

The 15th century, when the English language entered its modern period, is close in time to the beginning of the English Renaissance. The Renaissance started in England in the 16th century (later than it did in Italy) and was precipitated by several important events.

An important catalyst for the English Renaissance came from developments in technology. Around 1455, Johannes Gutenberg, the inventor of moveable type, produced the first printed book—the Gutenberg Bible. In 1474, William Caxton set up the first printing press in England. Caxton's press made books available to people from all walks of life and caused a veritable information revolution in Renaissance England.

Another important achievement was in the military sphere. In 1588, the mighty Spanish fleet, called the Armada, sailed to the coast of England with the intent of overthrowing Queen Elizabeth I. The victory of the 130 ships of the Armada over the 34 smaller English ships seemed predestined. But the English sailors not only managed to torch the Spanish fleet, they also benefitted from an improbable stroke of luck. A sudden storm lashed the fleeing Spaniards, crushing their boats against the rocky cliffs of England. After the Armada had been destroyed, England was poised to emerge as the world's major seafaring power.

The ambitious and brilliant Queen Elizabeth I became the most successful and beloved English monarch. She has given her first name to an entire era: the English Renaissance is also known as the Elizabethan Age. The gutsy and daring Elizabethans were driven by insatiable curiosity and ambition. During this period, English seamen raced across the oceans as far as Africa and the Americas, bringing home a wealth of new products and experiences.

The exchange of commodities and ideas resulted in a huge explosion of vocabulary. Hundreds of foreign words became part of the English language. Some new words that the Elizabethans picked up during their seafaring exploits were the French *chocolate* (originally the Nahuatl *chocolatl*) and the Italian *carnival*; the Spanish and Portuguese *alligator, anchovy, apricot, guitar, hammock,* and *hurricane*; the Persian *bazaar* and *caravan*; the Turkish *coffee* and *kiosk*; and the Dutch *landscape* and *knapsack*.

Many more new words were created by scholars. Because Renaissance scholars were inspired by the Greek and Latin philosophers, they turned to these ancient languages when coining words for new concepts. Among the learned terms that have entered English via classical sources are *anonymous, appropriate, atmosphere, concept, invention, lexicon, manuscript, pneumonia, radius, specimen, tendon, thermometer, transcribe, utopian,* and *virus,* to name just a few. Most English scientific terms are of either Greek or Latin origin.

Modern English also owes a huge number of words to the creative genius of Queen Elizabeth's most famous subject, William Shakespeare. Shakespeare's word coinages, which once sounded from the stages of the crowded Elizabethan theaters, are still in use today. In these words one discerns the spirit of innovation typical of the English Renaissance. Just consider some of the phrases created by Shakespeare: *the be-all and end-all, fast and loose, budge an inch, leap frog, lackluster, more in sorrow than in anger, thin air.*

Times of social transformation are generally accompanied by pronunciation changes. One such change affected Early Modern English. Recall that, in Old English, long vowels had a continental pronunciation. In early Modern English, however, the long vowels took on new value. All the English long vowels underwent this transformation. Thus, *see* was no longer pronounced "sehh," *house* stopped being pronounced "hoohs," and *moon* was not "mohn" anymore. Instead, the Old English long vowels either ended up being fronted or else turned into diphthongs. This phenomenon went down in history under the name of the *Great Vowel Shift.* This change in the value of long vowels started in the Middle English period has continued until modern times, as the vowels have slowly developed their current pronunciation.

The Great Vowel Shift is the reason behind irregularities of English spelling. The timing of the shift was peculiar. It was in progress in the 15th century, when the printing press had already been invented, and English spelling was being standardized. While English pronunciation continued to change, the spelling system had already become fixed. In this way, English ended up with a pre-shift spelling system and post-shift pronunciation.

Figure 11.1 provides a snapshot of major changes in the English language.

OE	ME	EME
	loss of inflections	Great Vowel Shift
5th c., Anglo-Saxon invasion	1066, Norman Invasion	1476, introduction of printing 1588, defeat of the Armada

Figure 11.1   English language change timeline.

Attitudes Toward Language Change

You now know that English has undergone some profound changes. But how have people felt about them?

Quite often, language change creeps up on us inconspicuously; language users do not necessarily register a pronunciation fad or a new grammatical structure. When people do notice a change, though, they tend to view it with resentment.

Consider the Inkhorn Controversy, which erupted when a stream of Greek and Latin terms, such as *anonymous, appropriate, atmosphere, concept,* and *invention,* poured into the English language through the writings of Renaissance scholars. Some prominent thinkers were outraged by the new borrowings, calling them "inkhorn" words. (An "inkhorn" was a small vessel for holding ink; the term implied that only learned writers would use such words.) Loan-word detractors argued that Latin and Greek-based neologisms were counterfeit concoctions that made English incomprehensible. They alleged that attorneys, government officials, and other men of power purposefully made their language obscure in order to intimidate ordinary people and to erect barriers of communication between themselves and others.

Loan-word proponents, meanwhile, argued that borrowing words from classical sources would augment and enrich English. George Pettie, a supporter of borrowings, angrily defended the use of new words, suggesting that "if they [the new borrowed words] should be all counted inkpot tearmes, I know not how we should speake anie thing without blacking our mouthes." Sometimes even those who were enthusiastic about neologisms felt a little guilty about using them. One writer felt compelled to apologize for the use of the word *maturity* in his writing, describing the new term as "strange and dark." But he hastened to assure his readers that the word would soon become "as facile to vnderstande as other words late commen out of Italy and France." In the long run, the campaign against neologisms proved futile. Most Latinate terms caught on, and Latin-based terms today constitute the core of the English scientific vocabulary.

And yet, in the 18th century, during the age of Enlightenment, the debate about language change flared up with new force. Men of that age had the highest regard for human reason and sought to improve society by establishing rational, authoritative laws. They wished to improve not only the social order, but even language itself. One of the most zealous language reformers was Jonathan Swift, the author of the world-renowned *Gulliver's Travels.* Swift, a man of censorious disposition, was dismayed by speech mannerisms that he considered careless and pretentious. For instance, he detested the clipping of the words *reputation* and *positive* into *rep* and *pos.* (If Swift were alive today, he probably wouldn't like the words *chem* and *prof.*) He hated words that he saw as mere fads, such as *sham, banter,* or *bully,* and he detested the new, contracted pronunciation of the *-ed* ending—in which speakers left out the *e* sound and said "rebuk'd," "disturb'd," and "drudg'd," not "rebukid," "disturbid," and "drudgid." To combat language corruption, Swift composed a "Proposal for Correcting, Improving and Ascertaining the English Tongue," in which he called for the creation of a language academy (similar to that in France) that would determine and maintain proper English grammar and pronunciation. No such academy was founded, however, and the pronunciation patterns, as well as many of the words, that Swift found unpalatable have come into everyday use.

In 1755, Dr. Samuel Johnson, another renowned figure of the English Enlightenment, published the first comprehensive English dictionary. Originally, Dr. Johnson conceived of the dictionary as a means of fixing and standardizing English so that the language "may be preserved, its use ascertained and its duration lengthened." But, as Dr. Johnson continued his work, he changed his mind. In the preface to his dictionary, he wrote the following famous words:

> When we see men grow old and die at a certain time one after another, from century to century, we laugh at the elixir that promises to prolong life to a thousand years; and with equal justice may the lexicographer be derided, who being able to produce no example of a nation that has preserved their words and phrases from mutability, shall imagine that his dictionary can embalm his language.

English language history provides ample evidence that Dr. Johnson was right. Purists who feel that phonological and grammatical changes happen because speakers are sloppy with language have been unable to stop the language from changing.

Today, professionals' and laymen's attitudes to language change are often at variance. Linguists, who tend to see the bigger picture and know that the English language has survived the Norman Conquest, French and Latin borrowings, profound grammatical restructuring, and the Great Vowel Shift, see language change as inevitable, a precondition of language growth. Laymen tend to feel more protective about language. They often express concerns that a new word, pronunciation pattern, or grammatical form will lead to language deterioration.

Modern English: A Global Lingua Franca

The history of Modern English has been a history of expansion. As a result of England's colonial activity, English became the mother tongue of a great number of people in the United States, Canada, Ireland, Australia, New Zealand, South Africa, and some Caribbean countries. Even after the British Empire crumbled, English retained the special status of a second official or compromise language in over 70 states, including Ghana, Nigeria, India, Hong Kong, and Singapore.

Today, a new change is affecting English: it is gradually emerging as a global lingua franca, a common language used for communication by people of diverse language backgrounds. The role that English plays in international communication is without precedent. Unlike Latin, Russian, Arabic, or Spanish (the lingua francas of the past, whose dominance used to be limited to certain regions), English is on its way to becoming the first common language of the entire world. It is estimated that about half of the world's population (approximately 4 billion people) has some knowledge of English.[2]

Because translation-related expenses are prohibitive, international bodies such as the United Nations, UNICEF, UNESCO, the World Health Organization, and the European Union are under pressure to use English as the single language of communication. English has also emerged as the chief language of trade and commerce. Indian call centers, for instance, rely on the use of English.

At the same time, English is the dominant language of popular culture. In 1994, 80% of all released feature films were in English.[3] English-language productions such as *Jurassic Park*, *Aladdin*, and *Avatar* have been international blockbusters. English is also the primary language of popular music. Out of the 557 pop groups listed in *The Penguin Encyclopedia of Popular Music*, 549 (99%) work entirely or predominantly in English.[4]

English has also evolved as the primary language for storing and sharing information. According to some estimates, 80% of the world's information is couched in English.[5] English is the main language in use on the Internet and in electronic communications. Within 3 years of its founding in 2000, the English-language site Wikipedia (from Hawaiian *wiki*, meaning "quick," and classical Greek *paideia*, meaning "education") scored 2–3 billion hits a month![6] Increasingly, scientists throughout the world publish their studies in English. Even in the research field of linguistics, which is sensitive to language issues, papers tend to be written in English. David Crystal, a linguist who has written a book about the global spread of English, reports that

90% of the studies listed in the journal *Linguistics Abstracts* are written in English—and that the trend is even larger in computer science.[7]

Because of the important economic and social advantages offered by a command of English, many countries have been promoting English-language instruction. English is the most widely taught foreign language in over 100 countries, including Russia, Germany, Spain, Egypt, and Brazil. Particularly notable has been its growth in the countries of the former Soviet Union, where it is thought that 10% of the population—10 million people—are now learning English. Countries such as Latvia, Estonia, and Lithuania, where the teaching of Russian used to be mandatory due to the Soviet Union's Russification policies, have switched to teaching English as the primary foreign language. Similar processes have taken place in Africa. In 1996, English replaced French as the chief foreign language in Algeria, a former French colony.

Some countries have even introduced English at the elementary-school level. In 2006, English was added to the Mexican primary-school curriculum as a mandatory second language, prompting 200,000 Mexican schoolteachers to enroll in English-language teaching programs.[8] In Taiwan and South Korea, elementary-level English-as-a-foreign-language (EFL) programs have been created. Dubbed "English villages," these programs provide students with immersion experiences by placing them in a realistic English-language environment. For instance, in a school in Taiwan, a classroom was transformed to look like an airport waiting room and customs area, complete with a genuine plane fuselage donated by a Taiwanese airline company. In another Taiwanese "English village," foreign volunteer teachers interact with young students.[9] In the Indian state of Bihar, young schoolchildren receive their EFL lessons over the radio. The state government gives each elementary school 1,000 rupees ($25) for the purchase of a radio, enabling the 122-episode program "English is Fun" to reach an enthusiastic young audience.[10] In Hong Kong, South Korea, Taiwan, and Malaysia, huge audiences of young viewers enjoy EFL television programs featuring a cartoon character named Noddy.[11]

There is also growing interest in learning English among the adolescent and adult population worldwide. For example, in China in the wake of the 2008 Olympic Games, the charismatic teacher Li Young taught English to an audience of thousands of professionals, under the slogan "Conquer English to Make China Strong!"[12]

Students sometimes wonder if Chinese, Spanish, or some other language is likely to become the world's next lingua franca. This is not the place to make long-term predictions about language change—and such predictions seldom prove accurate anyhow. The short-term perspective, however, seems clear. At the moment, English enjoys too much of a head start for its dominant status to be threatened. In the near future, English will probably continue to spread—and so will interest in learning it.

Implications for Instruction

1. Knowledge of language change can help language teachers explain some difficult points of English spelling and grammar. Given that the spelling of English words reflects their pre-Great Vowel Shift pronunciation, how can you explain the current pronunciation of the letter *a* and the silent *e* in the words *name* and *take*?

2. While the [k] and [g] sounds in the words *knight, know,* and *gnat* used to be pronounced in Old English, these (and other) consonants have become silent in Modern English. Given this pattern, how would you explain to your students why the initial *w* consonant in *write* is silent?

3. Taking Old English stem-vowel mutation and ablaut into account, how would you explain to students the irregular plurals and past tenses of English nouns and verbs?

4. The tendency on the part of some students (and native speakers) to drop the ending *-s* in the third-person singular of the verb—resulting in utterances such as *He go there*—is consistent with morphological processes that have been in evidence since the early days of English language history. As a language teacher, what stance are you going to take with respect to this error?

5. Conduct a study to further your understanding of EFL or ESL instruction in a foreign country or an immigrant community. What purposes do students pursue in studying English? What economic and social gains will mastery of English provide? Does English threaten the status of the community's first language?

6. Just as the invention of print did in the Middle Ages, the Internet revolution is likely to have a profound impact on language. Observe language changes that are brought about by new technological tools and discuss how you are going to account for these changes in your classroom.

SOME WORDS TO REMEMBER

Old English: the form of English used from the 5th century a.d. until the Norman Invasion of 1066.

Anglo-Saxon language: see **Old English**.

Middle English: the form of English used in the Middle Ages from 1066 until the 15th century.

Modern English: the form of English used from the 15th-century start of the Renaissance period until today.

continental pronunciation: the pattern of vowel pronunciation whereby spelling and pronunciation match each other.

inflected languages: languages that have a rich system of bound morphemes (e.g., Old English).

vowel mutation: the process of forming the plural form of nouns via changes in the stem vowel (e.g., *goose/geese*).

ablaut: the process of forming the past tense of verbs via changes in the stem vowel (e.g., *bring/brought*).

leveling of inflections: the process of losing endings.

falling together of inflections: see **leveling of inflections**.

Great Vowel Shift: the change in the quality of long vowels in Early Modern English.

Inkhorn Controversy: the debate during the English Renaissance over the use of borrowed Greek and Latin terms.

lingua franca: a common language used for communication by people of diverse language backgrounds.

Notes

1. Leech, G. (2003). Modality on the move: The English modal auxiliaries 1961–1992. In R. Facchinetti, M. Krug, & F. R. Palmer (Eds.), *Modality in contemporary English*. Berlin: Mouton de Gruyter.
2. McCrum, R. (2010). *Globish: How the English language became the world's language*. New York: W.W. Norton.
3. *Film and Television Handbook*. (1996). Cited in Crystal, D. (1997). *English as a global language*. Cambridge, UK: Cambridge University Press.
4. Crystal, D. (1997). *English as a global language*. Cambridge, UK: Cambridge University Press.
5. Ibid.
6. McCrum, R. (2010). *Globish: How the English language became the world's language*. New York: W.W. Norton.
7. Crystal, D. (1997). *English as a global language*. Cambridge, UK: Cambridge University Press.

8. McCrum, R. (2010). *Globish: How the English language became the world's language*. New York: W.W. Norton.
9. Gluck, C. (2007). English village opens in Taiwan. *BBC News*. Retrieved from http://news.bbc.co.uk/2/hi/uk_news/education/6992823.stm.
10. Tewary, A. (2008). English radio lessons a hit in India. *BBC News*. Retrieved from http://news.bbc.co.uk/2/hi/7391742.stm.
11. Noddy goes back to school. (2003). *BBC News*. Retrieved from http://news.bbc.co.uk/2/hi/business/3237399.stm.
12. Osnos, E. (2008, April 28). Letter from China. *The New Yorker*.

About the Author

Tatiana Gordon studied linguistics and methodology at St. Petersburg Pedagogical University in Russia, taught English in the St. Petersburg elementary school and then became a professor of linguistics at her alma mater. In 1989, she emigrated to the United States. While working as a New York City public school teacher, she won several awards for excellence in teaching. Upon completing her doctoral research in applied linguistics at Teachers College, Columbia University, she has been teaching linguistics and methodology at Hofstra University in Hempstead, New York. A number of her professional publications have focused on linking linguistic research to classroom practice.